Real T...

Authe...

D0765104

Teacher's Manual
with Answer Key
and Tests

Lida Baker
Judith Tanka

PEARSON
Longman

Real Talk 2
Teacher's Manual with Answer Key and Tests

Pearson Education, 10 Bank Street, White Plains, NY 10606

Staff credits: The people who made up the **Real Talk 2 Teacher's Manual with Answer
Key and Tests** team, representing editorial, production, design, and manufacturing,
are Danielle Belfiore, Elizabeth Carlson, Christine Edmonds, Nancy Flaggman,
Amy McCormick, Kathleen Silloway, and Paula Van Ells.

Text composition: Laserwords
Text font: 11/13 Times

ISBN-10: 0-13-194097-X
ISBN-13: 978-0-13-194097-0

Printed in the United States of America

LONGMAN ON THE **WEB**

Pearsonlongman.com offers online resources
for teachers and students. Access our
Companion Websites, our online catalog, and
our local offices around the world.

Visit us at **pearsonlongman.com**.

CONTENTS

INTRODUCTION TO *REAL TALK 2*

LEVEL AND AUDIENCE

Real Talk 2 is a textbook for English-language learners that employs authentic listening passages in a variety of real-world contexts as the basis for the development of listening and speaking skills. The text is designed for adult and young adult learners at the advanced level in both second- and foreign-language environments. (This Teacher's Manual includes explanatory notes and suggestions for the benefit of teachers located both inside and outside the United States.)

A companion text, *Real Talk 1*, is aimed at the high-intermediate level.

AUDIO

The audio material for this book consists of recordings of "real" people (not actors) speaking in four real-world contexts: in person, on the phone, on the air, and in class. The recordings include features such as false starts, fillers, hesitations, repetitions, and errors, all of which are integral parts of authentic speech. By means of carefully structured and sequenced exercises, the book teaches students how to recognize the essential information in the messy stream of sound they encounter in the real English-speaking world.

CHAPTER CONTENT AND ORGANIZATION

Real Talk 2 consists of eight chapters, each of which is organized around a general theme, such as money or movies. Each chapter is then divided into four parts, corresponding to—and named after—the four contexts in which spoken English normally occurs, that is, In Person, On the Phone, On the Air, and In Class. The following is a brief description of the recordings in each part:

    Part 1, In Person: Face-to-face conversations and interviews.
    Part 2, On the Phone: Personal and business-related phone conversations as well as authentic recorded announcements like the automated "menu" at a movie theater.
    Part 3, On the Air: Excerpts from a variety of radio programs, including both news and feature segments.
    Part 4, In Class: Academic mini-lectures, typically six to eight minutes in length.

Each chapter part above is divided into prelistening, listening, and postlistening sections. Exercises target vocabulary development, listening for main ideas, details and inferences, pronunciation, language functions, and note-taking.

SPEAKING ACTIVITIES

All sections (prelistening, listening, postlistening) of each chapter part include speaking activities. Most skill-building work is done in pairs or small groups, and students normally go over answers to exercises with their classmates. The postlistening section, called Real Talk: Use What You've Learned, includes a vocabulary review and communication activities that provide students with the opportunity to practice the language skills and features presented in that part.

A special feature of **Real Talk 2** is a TOEFL® practice activity at the end of each In Class section. Modeled after the TOEFL iBT, this section requires students to synthesize information from a lecture and a related short reading and to prepare an oral presentation in response to a prompt.

For a detailed description of the exercises and activities within each section and suggestions for teaching them, see the General Teaching Tips on pages 3–15.

TEACHING SEQUENCE AND TIME MANAGEMENT

The listening and speaking skills presented in **Real Talk 2** loosely build on one another from part to part and from chapter to chapter, especially in the first three chapters. (See the Scope and Sequence in the front of the Student Book for details.) We recommend teaching at least the early chapters in sequence. Nevertheless, it is possible to skip chapters or parts of chapters in order to accommodate the interests and needs of your students. The book also lends itself to some independent study. For example, if you have some students who will be attending an English-speaking university and others who will not, you could assign Part Four: In Class to the university-bound students to do in the listening lab.

Every class is different, so it is not possible for us to state precisely how much time you will need in order to cover each chapter of **Real Talk 2**. In our field-testing of the materials, Parts One, Two, and Three required between one and two hours of class time to complete. Part Four required between two and three hours. You can reduce the class time needed by assigning some activities, such as the vocabulary work in the pre- and post-listening sections, for homework.

We hope **Real Talk 2** will be an engaging and practical vehicle for enabling your students to reach the next level in their English-language acquisition.

L.B. and J.T.

GENERAL TEACHING TIPS

Parts One to Three

Parts One to Three (In Person, On the Phone, and On the Air) have similar organization and components, described in this section. Part Four: In Class is somewhat different and is described separately in the section that follows.

A. PRELISTENING

Each chapter part opens with a prelistening section consisting of three items:

- art;
- a speaking activity;
- a vocabulary preview.

Keeping in mind that students will probably be eager to get to the listening, we advise spending no more than twenty or thirty minutes on prelistening work.

Art

Visuals consist of items related to the content of the listening, such as photographs, drawings, graphs, or cartoons. The purpose of the art is to tap into students' previous knowledge and to stimulate their curiosity regarding the upcoming listening. Note that many pieces of art do not have captions, so it is important that students look at the art and discuss it before listening.

SUGGESTED PROCEDURE
Begin the lesson by having students look at the art. Ask questions such as the following:

- What do you see?
- How does this (photo, graph, etc.) relate to your previous experience?
- What information does it convey?
- How does it make you feel?
- Based on the art, what do you think the listening will be about?

Speaking Activity

This activity, like the art, is designed to call up students' prior knowledge of the listening topic and to motivate them to listen. Most often the activity consists of discussion, but there are also quizzes and surveys in some chapters. The directions always state the general topic of the upcoming listening and specify how students should be grouped.

SUGGESTED PROCEDURE
1. Go over the directions and group students as directed. Give an approximate time limit for the activity.
2. Circulate while students are working. Answer questions and provide help as needed.

(continued)

3. When time is up, bring the class back together and wrap up the activity by summarizing answers that seemed to recur from group to group, mentioning one or two unusual comments you heard, or correcting errors. You can also ask one person from each group to summarize that group's discussion.

Vocabulary Preview

In this exercise, students read a list of key words and expressions from the listening. Working alone or in pairs, they check off the items they already know. They should check off the remaining words as they learn them throughout the chapter part. The goal is for students to have checked off all the items on the list by the time they complete the chapter part.

OPTIONAL PROCEDURE
1. Read the items aloud and have students repeat so that they can match the spelling of the words with their pronunciation.
2. Assign the Vocabulary Preview as homework to be completed before doing the listening work (see Listening, below). This is one way to save time in class.

B. LISTENING

There are three activities in this section, arranged from global to specific.

Main Ideas

Students listen to the entire recording once and answer questions targeting the main ideas of the listening. Question types include multiple choice, fill-in, true/false, and open-ended questions that students answer in note form. Even students at this advanced level should be reassured that they don't need to understand every word in order to comprehend the main ideas. They will be well prepared for listening if they have done the prelistening speaking and vocabulary activities.

SUGGESTED PROCEDURE
1. Go over the directions with the class.
2. Instruct students to read the questions before listening. This will help them to focus their listening. Encourage them to predict the answers on the basis of the prelistening activities they have already done.
3. Play the recording. Students may answer questions while listening, but give them time afterward to finish.
4. Play the recording again if necessary.
5. In general, do not allow students to read the audioscript while they are listening. You may want to make an exception for students whose listening ability is markedly lower than that of most of the students in the class.
6. After listening, have students work in pairs and compare their answers, or go over the answers with the whole class.

Details and Inferences

Some of the questions in this section target details from the listening. Other questions require students to draw inferences or guess the meaning of vocabulary by using the context.

Suggested Procedure

1. Go over the directions with the class.
2. Give students time to read the questions before listening. If they know the answers from their earlier listening, they may answer the questions now and check them when they listen again.
3. Play the recording. As in the Main Ideas section, students may begin answering questions as they listen, but give them time afterward to finish.
4. Have students work in pairs and have them compare and discuss their answers, or go over the answers with the whole class.
5. A useful strategy to employ when going over inference questions is to ask students "How do you know?" This question requires them to explain which pieces of information led them to the answer they chose. In this way you can check that they did not get the correct answer by chance.
6. If students are unable to answer a question, replay the section of the recording containing the information they need. Stop the recording at that point and ask students to repeat what they heard. Ask additional questions to help students understand, but do not allow them to read the audioscript except as a last resort. (See Using the Audioscript, page 14.)

Listening for Language

This section targets specific features of spoken English and presents explanations and exercises in a bottom-up fashion. Two kinds of activities are presented. (Most chapter parts include both types; a few contain one or the other.) The first, Focus on Sound, targets phonological features such as stress and reductions; and the second, Conversation Tools, deals with functions or semantic groups (such as banking terms). The teaching points were selected on the basis of their occurrence and prominence in the listening.

Focus on Sound

This section begins with an explanation of the phonological feature, such as linking and blending, followed by a focused listening exercise. Some exercise items are extracted directly from the recording. Others have been written and recorded for the specific instructional purpose of the exercise. Listening is normally followed by controlled speaking practice with the targeted pronunciation feature.

Suggested Procedure

1. Read or have students read the explanation of the pronunciation feature.
2. Model the examples in the explanation. Check to make sure students have understood the explanation and the terminology used.
3. Play the recording and have students complete the task. If the task calls for students to repeat after the speaker, encourage everyone to participate. If pauses between items appear inadequate, lengthen the time by using the pause button on your audio equipment.
4. Do not insist on native-like pronunciation. It is more important for students to be able to comprehend what they hear than to reproduce it precisely.
5. Have students work in pairs and compare their answers to the exercises, or go over the answers with the whole class.

CONVERSATION TOOLS

This section begins with a list of functions (called *conversation tools* because they are used for specific communicative purposes) and an explanation of their proper use and cultural context. The list is followed by a focused listening and/or speaking activity in which students practice the function being presented.

SUGGESTED PROCEDURE

1. Read or have students read the list of functions. Model the correct pronunciation and have students repeat. Explain unfamiliar vocabulary if necessary. Note that many functions are idiomatic expressions and therefore cannot be translated word for word. For example, the expression "slip one's mind," taught in Chapter 4, has a very different meaning from the literal meaning of the words "slip" or "mind."
2. Have students complete the listening or speaking task that follows. Monitor pairs or groups to ensure they are using the language properly.

C. REAL TALK: USE WHAT YOU'VE LEARNED

This section includes a vocabulary review and one or more communicative speaking activities that incorporate the skills and language presented in the previous two sections. The speaking activities include discussions, role plays, community surveys, debates, and oral presentations.

Vocabulary Review

SUGGESTED PROCEDURE

1. Read or have students read the directions. Have them form pairs as indicated. This activity can also be done in small groups.
2. Chapter 1, page 6, in the Student Book has a list of Steps for Reviewing Vocabulary. Refer students back to this list as needed.

OPTIONAL HOMEWORK

For additional practice with the new vocabulary, assign one of the following tasks:

* Have students write their own sentences using the new vocabulary. This can be done on paper or in a vocabulary notebook, which students turn in periodically for you to check.
* Have students write a composition related to the theme of the chapter part. Encourage them to use as much of the new vocabulary as possible.
* Have students use a search engine or an online concordance and record examples of authentic uses of the vocabulary. (For help, see the article "The Compleat Lexical Tutor" in the *TESL E-J*, http://www-writing.berkeley.edu/TESL-EJ/ej31/m2.html.)

Discussions

Nearly every part of every chapter includes a discussion activity in which students share their own experiences and opinions about the topic of the lesson. Early in the course, you should review expressions for interrupting, asking for repetition, and keeping the conversation going. (See *Real Talk 1,* Chapter 3, page 59; *Real Talk 2*, Chapter 2, page 40.)

1. Read the directions and place students in pairs or groups. To ensure that discussions stay on task, clearly state the goal or purpose of the activity and give students a time limit in which to accomplish the goal.
2. Emphasize that everyone needs to participate in the discussion. It may be helpful to assign roles to group members. For example, there can be a leader, who keeps the group on task and makes sure everyone has a chance to speak; a secretary, who takes notes; a reporter, whose job is to summarize the discussion and report on it to the rest of the class; a timekeeper; and a "vocabulary monitor," who encourages group members to use new vocabulary from the lesson wherever possible.
3. Remind students to look back at the vocabulary list for the chapter part and try, as much as possible, to use new words from the list.
4. As students are talking, circulate and monitor the discussion. Answer questions and take notes on items you want to go over when the discussion is finished.
5. Leave a few minutes at the end to bring the class back together and wrap up the discussion. Use this time to make comments, answer questions, go over errors, or have a student from each group report on the results of the group's discussion.

Role Plays

This type of activity presents students with scenarios in which they assume roles and act out situations in pairs, in groups, or in front of the whole class.

SUGGESTED PROCEDURE
1. When possible, bring in props or costumes to add drama and fun to the role play. Advanced learners appreciate these touches just as much as beginning ones do.
2. As always, begin by reading the directions. Follow the directions for grouping students and assigning roles.
3. If students are not familiar with role playing, act out a sample one with an outgoing volunteer. If another demonstration is needed, have two students do it.
4. Give students plenty of time to plan their role play and rehearse. Students may make notes, but they should not write out complete scripts.
5. While students are preparing, circulate, answer questions, and offer suggestions.
6. If students perform their role plays in front of the whole class, begin by calling for volunteers.
7. If your class is large, students can perform their role plays for one or two other pairs or groups.

OPTIONAL PROCEDURE
1. If you plan to have students perform their role plays in front of the class, have one pair practice with another pair before doing it in front of the whole group.
2. An option for highly fluent and outgoing students is to perform their role play extemporaneously, i.e., with no time to rehearse.
3. Once students are very familiar and comfortable with role playing, record or videotape their role plays and have them listen to or view themselves "in action."
4. Do not give students grades on role plays. However, take notes on both correct and incorrect uses of the language features being practiced and offer both praise and correction.

In these speaking activities, students gather information from each other—or, if possible, from English speakers outside their class—using a set of questions provided in the Student Book or written by the students themselves. For surveys in which students talk with more than one person, a chart is usually provided in which they can take notes on the answers they collect.

Some activities ask students to interview English speakers. If that is not possible, do one of the following:

* Have students interview you and/or other English-speaking teachers at your school.
* Have them interview people they know who do not speak English, but instruct students to record in English the answers they collect and to report on the answers in class in English.

SUGGESTED PROCEDURE

Follow the detailed instructions in the Student Book for grouping students, preparing the questions, carrying out the interview or survey (in class or out), and following up with the whole class.

OPTIONAL PROCEDURE

As a follow-up, have students write compositions about the questions they asked, the answers they collected, and their opinion or interpretation of the responses they heard.

Oral Reports or Presentations

In this activity, students do research and plan an oral report or presentation.

SUGGESTED PROCEDURE

1. Allow students adequate time to prepare. If research is involved, we advise giving students at least a week to prepare their presentations.
2. Depending on the complexity of the presentation, you may have students prepare in stages as follows, and you may wish to check students' work at each step:
   * topic selection;
   * research;
   * rough outline;
   * final outline;
   * oral practice (in pairs or small groups);
   * presentation to the whole class.
3. Advise students that while speaking they may consult their outlines or use index cards, but they may not read from a fully written-out report. (As always, you may make an exception for students with lower-than-average speaking skills.) Students also should not memorize their presentations.
4. Allow for feedback on the presentations. You may use or adapt the Peer Evaluation Sheet on page 9.

PEER EVALUATION SHEET

NAME OF SPEAKER _____

TOPIC _____ DATE _____

	Excellent	Good	Fair	Poor
Organization				
Clarity (loudness, pronunciation, speed)				
Body language (eye contact, gestures, movement)				
Interest for you				
Use of media (handouts, computers, etc.)				
Overall grade				

Main point of presentation:

_____

_____

Two questions to ask this speaker:

_____

_____

Comments or suggestions for this speaker:

_____

_____

_____

Information Gaps

In these activities, students in pairs or groups are given different or partial sets of information. This creates a "gap" in the knowledge that different participants have. Students must speak to one another in order to piece together a complete set of information.

Suggested Procedure
1. Follow the instructions in the Student Book for grouping students and carrying out the activity. The information for Student A will usually be found on the same page as the instructions for the activity. The information for Student B (and occasionally Student C) will be found at the end of the chapter.
2. Remind students not to show one another their information.
3. While students are talking, circulate, provide help as needed, and monitor students' language use. Note significant errors.
4. When students finish, each person should have a complete set of data. Partners or group members should look at one another's papers to make sure they got everything right.
5. Bring the class back together and discuss any interesting or unusual facts that emerged from the activity.

Part Four

In this part of the chapter, In Class, students hear an academic mini-lecture and learn how to take notes. At the beginning of the course, take a few moments to explain why note-taking is important. Students who plan to study at a North American university will need to use their lecture notes whenever they study for a test because exams include information from both lectures and books. Non-academic students will also benefit from note-taking because the process of listening and taking notes requires students to think in English, which in turn helps them to develop their fluency in the language.

A. PRELISTENING

This section consists of activities similar to those in Parts One to Three. Students are asked to respond to a visual prompt (such as a photo, graph, or drawing), discuss their background knowledge about the topic, and complete a vocabulary preview exercise. The purpose of these activities is to elicit interest in the lecture topic, to allow students to share what they already know about it, and to provide essential language that they will need in order to comprehend the content of the lecture. For additional instructions, see the recommended procedures under Prelistening, pages 3–4.

B. LISTENING AND NOTE-TAKING

This section begins with a presentation of one or more academic note-taking skills, which are determined by the particular organization and language of the lecture. This focused skill work prepares students for

- the organizational pattern of the lecture they will hear (cause and effect, pro-con, etc.);
- the language (specific expressions) that provides cues to the speaker's organization;
- the form of the lecture notes that students need to take—generally an outline.

These three items are taught in sections called Lecture Organization, Lecture Language, and Lecture Note Form, respectively.

Lecture Organization

This section begins with an explanation of the organizational structure or pattern used in the lecture. Examples include definition, cause and effect, and the organization of research studies and scientific processes. After reading the explanation, students do a listening task focusing on the pattern taught.

SUGGESTED PROCEDURE
1. Read or have students read the explanation.
2. Read the directions to the listening task.
3. Play the recording and monitor students as they complete the task. Some exercises may require that you pause the recording between items. Depending on your students' level of comprehension, you may want to extend the pauses or replay some items if necessary.
4. It is often helpful to stop the recording after students have done the first item and check that they are doing the task correctly.
5. After listening, have students share and compare their answers in pairs. Encourage them to discuss the reasons for their answers.

Lecture Language

This section teaches commonly used words and phrases that are associated with lectures in general and specific organizational patterns in particular. Examples include cohesive devices (such as pronoun reference), verbs associated with statistics and numbers, language for talking about hypothetical situations, and expressions of contrast. Learning such language will greatly enhance students' ability to predict and comprehend lecture content.

The teaching material consists of an explanation and a list of words and phrases, followed by a listening exercise based on one or more excerpts from the lecture. Students must recognize and/or use the words and phrases from the list in order to complete the task.

SUGGESTED PROCEDURE
Follow the recommended procedures described under Lecture Organization, above.

Lecture Note Form

Here students learn the basics of efficient note-taking, such as outlining and taking notes on statistics. A list of commonly used symbols and abbreviations is included in Appendix 2 of the Student Book, page 221, but you should encourage students to develop their own system of "telegraphic" writing. In addition, feel free to allow students to take notes in ways other than the traditional outline form. Some other ways of arranging notes on a page may include using columns, boxes, or some other visual representation of relationships between ideas. (Graphic note form is taught in Chapter 2.) An Internet search for *graphic organizers* will yield a wide variety of scaffolds for taking notes. The goal is for students to be able to note important information in a clear and comprehensible way that will enable them to recall key points.

Follow the recommended procedures described under Lecture Organization, page 11.

Taking Notes

In this activity, students hear the entire lecture and practice the note-taking skills they have learned. In the real world, note-taking is a two-step process: Students take notes on their own paper, then edit and rewrite their notes. We follow a similar procedure in this text. First students listen to the lecture and take notes on their own paper. Afterward, they rewrite their notes by filling in the incomplete scaffold in the Student Book. The amount of scaffolding provided decreases from the beginning of the book until the end. This procedure may appear unconventional, but we have found it to be an effective way to teach students to take accurate, well-organized notes.

SUGGESTED PROCEDURE

1. Read or call on a student to read the directions. Before listening, have students look at the incomplete outline and the listening cues provided in the margin. Also have students examine any visuals that accompany the lecture. Tell them to pay special attention to
   - the overall form and organization of the lecture;
   - what information is already in the outline;
   - what key points to listen for, as indicated by the margin notes.
2. Encourage students to make predictions about what they will hear.
3. Remind students
   - to use all the note-taking skills taught up to that point;
   - to aim for understanding the key points rather than 100 percent of the lecture;
   - not to panic if they miss a major point, but instead to leave space in their notes because speakers often recycle information or summarize it in the conclusion.
4. Have students close their books. Play the recording and have students take notes on their own paper.
5. Replay sections that are difficult for the class.
6. After listening, have students edit and rewrite their notes using the outline in their book.

If students are having difficulty taking notes, especially in the early chapters of the book, the following techniques may be helpful.

- Model the process by playing the recording and writing notes on the board or an overhead projector transparency while students watch.
- Play the lecture more than once. Allow students to listen the first time without taking notes. Then play the recording again and have them take notes on their own paper.
- While students are listening to the lecture, pause the recording at regular intervals to give them time to restate what they heard, ask questions, or make predictions about what is coming next.
- Divide the class into groups and have each group take notes on just one part of the lecture. Afterward, have students share and combine their notes as they rewrite them in their books.

If you have students whose listening ability is significantly below that of the rest of the class, you can allow them either to read the lecture script ahead of time or read the script during the first listening. Then these students can listen again and take notes.

Reviewing the Lecture

The purpose of this section is

* to allow students to compare their notes with their classmates' and fill in information they may have missed;
* to check their comprehension by discussing and reacting to the lecture content.

SUGGESTED PROCEDURES

1. Read the directions and group students as directed.
2. Have students respond to the questions orally by referring to their notes. If key information is missing, they will not be able to answer and will need to consult their classmates. Monitor groups or pairs and note whether a large number of students missed the same information. If so, you may want to do one or more of the following:
   * provide the missing information to the whole class;
   * replay the segment of the lecture that contains the information they missed;
   * discuss with the class possible reasons why they missed the information the first time (unfamiliar vocabulary, speed of delivery, the complexity or unfamiliarity of the topic).
3. Refer students to Appendix 3 in the Student Book, pages 222–223, so that they may compare their notes to a "perfect" model. (But remind students that nobody's notes are perfect in the real world! The outlines were constructed based on written transcripts of the lectures. Even a native speaker would not have been able to take such perfect notes while listening.)
4. During the discussion portion of this follow-up activity, encourage students to share their personal perspectives about the lecture topic. Although some of the questions ask this directly, feel free to add more prompts such as:
   * Did you learn anything new or surprising in this lecture?
   * Do you agree with the lecturer's point of view? Which side of the issue presented here do you agree with?
   * What personal experience have you had with this subject?
5. Consult the audioscript or the Sample Outlines for In-Class Lecture in Appendix 4 of the Student Book for the answers to the questions in this section.

C. REAL TALK: USE WHAT YOU'VE LEARNED

This section contains activities similar to those in Parts One to Three: a Vocabulary Review and one or more communicative speaking activities that incorporate the skills and language presented in the previous two sections. The speaking activities include discussions, role plays, community surveys, debates, problem-solving tasks, and oral presentations.

For more specific instructions, see the recommended procedures under Real Talk: Use What You've Learned, pages 6–10.

TOEFL Practice: Synthesizing Listening, Reading, and Speaking

This section is designed to mirror the integrated speaking tasks on the TOEFL iBT. After completing the listening and note-taking activities in Part Four, students read a short passage with information that either supplements or contrasts with the topic of the lecture. Students then prepare a one-minute talk in response to a question that requires them to integrate information from both the lecture and the reading.

The suggested procedures below will help students to develop their test-taking skills. As students progress in the course, you should gradually eliminate these developmental steps so that students can complete the reading and speaking tasks in a manner that most closely imitates what they will be asked to do on the TOEFL.

SUGGESTED PROCEDURES

1. Have students read the passage either in class or at home. Doing it in class will more closely approximate an authentic testing situation.
2. *Optional*: Have students restate the main ideas of the reading in their own words.
3. Read the speaking prompt with the students and discuss ways to organize their talks. Have students prepare an outline alone, in pairs, or working as a whole class.
4. In the early part of the course, allow students to practice their talks before delivering them. They can practice alone at home or during class time with a partner.
5. To approximate test conditions as closely as possible, have students record their talks and turn them in to you.
6. TOEFL speaking tasks are scored on a scale from 0 to 4. You may wish to use the same system. To view the TOEFL iBT Speaking Task Scoring Rubrics, scroll to the end of this document: http://www.ets.org/Media/Tests/TOEFL/pdf/TOEFL_Tips.pdf.

Using the Audioscript

In this Teacher's Manual, we have already advised you strongly not to allow students to read the audioscript while they are listening. Having the option to read obviates the need to listen and undermines students' motivation. If, however, there are students in your class whose listening ability lags far behind that of their classmates, you may wish to give them the script to read *before* listening. Even these students, however, should be discouraged from listening and reading at the same time.

TIPS FOR USING THE AUDIOSCRIPT

1. We recommend that you listen to the recordings and read the audioscript before the lesson. This will help you to
   - become familiar with the context that students will be working with;
   - anticipate areas that may be difficult for students.

   Non-native English-speaking teachers who themselves may not have regular exposure to authentic spoken English may benefit most from this preparatory step.
2. Once students have completed the listening work in a chapter part, you may choose to allow them to read the audioscript and listen along. This gives many students—and teachers—a sense of completion at the end of a lesson.
3. Motivated students who wish to do more vocabulary work than is offered in the book may select additional items from the audioscript to learn.

Homework

Many of the prelistening and Real Talk: Use What You've Learned (post-listening) activities can be done outside of class. For example, we have suggested that the prelistening vocabulary exercise could be done at home prior to the listening lesson in order to save time in class. The following activities can also be done outside of class:

- Some of the Vocabulary Review exercises could be converted from interactive speaking activities to writing activities that students do on their own.
- In Part Four, the activity called Reviewing the Lecture could be assigned to groups of students or to individuals to do as homework.
- Most, if not all, surveys and interviews can be done outside of class.

The activities in the Listening section could be done independently in a listening lab, particularly if a student was absent and needs to make up the work. Nevertheless, because *Real Talk 2* is so highly interactive, we recommend covering as much of the material in class as possible.

Testing

This Teacher's Manual includes eight chapter tests, one for each chapter in *Real Talk 2*. The tests cover selected vocabulary, Conversation Tools, Focus on Sound, and Lecture Language segments.

Real Talk 2 Teacher's Manual **15**

CHAPTER
TEACHING
SUGGESTIONS

and

ANSWER KEY

TURNING POINTS

Part One: In Person

Background

- At most colleges in the United States, students are allowed to change their majors even after they have begun their studies. It is also becoming more and more common for people who have been working for a number of years to go back to school in order to begin a new career.
- In the past, most nurses in the United States were women. These days, many nurses are men.

Art

1. The photo shows the two speakers in this section, a young Korean-American woman named Carol and a young man named Scott.
2. See the General Teaching Tips, page 3, for suggestions on presenting art.

A. PRELISTENING (page 1)

See the General Teaching Tips, page 3, for suggestions on conducting prelistening speaking activities.

Discussion

1. See the General Teaching Tips, page 6, for suggestions on conducting discussions.
2. A *turning point* is an event or decision that changes a person's life in an important way.

Vocabulary Preview

See the General Teaching Tips, page 4, for suggestions on conducting the vocabulary preview.

B. LISTENING (page 2)
Main Ideas

See the General Teaching Tips, page 4, for suggestions on teaching the Main Ideas section.

🕐 ANSWERS

	Woman (Carol)	Man (Scott)
Major before switch	pre-med	math
Major after switch	religious studies	pre-med
Future career	minister	nurse
Reason for switch	It was her calling. She knew she would regret it if she didn't change.	Didn't want to spend his life dealing with formulas, abstract theories, numbers.

Details and Inferences

See the General Teaching Tips, page 4, for suggestions on teaching this section.

② ANSWERS

1. a. B; b. S; c. B; d. C; e. C; f. B

2. c

3. c. Her tone of voice conveys surprise.
Also, she says most nurses are women.

4. b

5. a. Asian families have high expectations
for their children's education.
b. Nurses work fewer hours than doctors,
so they have more free time.

6. 1. b
2. a
3. c
4. d

Listening for Language

See the General Teaching Tips, page 5, for suggestions on teaching this section.

FOCUS ON SOUND

1. See the General Teaching Tips, page 5, for suggestions on teaching Focus on Sound.
2. Some students may have trouble pronouncing a voiced /d/ at the end of a word. The usual error is to pronounce the ending as a /t/ or not to attach any past-tense marker at all. To teach students to pronounce a /d/ or any other voiced sound, instruct them to place their hands on their throats. Model some voiced sounds and have students repeat. Ask them if they feel anything in their throats; they should feel vibration. Then say some voiceless sounds, again have students repeat, and again ask what they feel; they should feel nothing. Next, have students do Exercise 4 with their hands on their throats. This will help them pronounce the final /d/.

CONVERSATION TOOLS

See the General Teaching Tips, page 6, for suggestions on teaching Conversation Tools.

⑦ SAMPLE ANSWERS
Answers will vary. For example:
Carol changed her mind about becoming a doctor.
She decided to change her major from pre-med to religious studies.
Scott switched gears and decided to become a nurse.
Both Scott and Carol switched their majors.
Scott started out as a math major.
Carol's family was surprised when she changed her major.

C. REAL TALK: USE WHAT YOU'VE LEARNED (page 6)
Vocabulary Review

1. See the General Teaching Tips, page 6, for suggestions on conducting the vocabulary review.
2. Be sure to circulate as students are talking. Note cases where students both correctly and incorrectly use the vocabulary being reviewed.

② ANSWERS

1. on the wrong track
2. *All the following are correct:* change directions; change my mind; go in a different direction; switch gears
3. (same as #2)
4. regret
5. started out
6. (same as #2)
7. made a decision; made up my mind
8. turning point
9. come about
10. supportive
11. compromise
12. in retrospect

Discussion

1. See the General Teaching Tips, page 6, for suggestions on conducting discussions.
2. The discussion may not generate all the words in the list on Student Book page 6. If you don't hear any examples of some items, ask students to make sentences with those items during the wrap-up phase of the activity.

Interview

1. See the General Teaching Tips, page 8, for suggestions on conducting interviews.
2. Elicit sample interview questions from the whole class and write them on the board.
3. *Optional:* Have students conduct the interviews in pairs. One student can ask the questions and the other can take notes on the answers.

Part Two: On the Phone

Art

See the General Teaching Tips, page 3, for suggestions on presenting art.

A. PRELISTENING (page 9)

See the General Teaching Tips, page 3, for suggestions on conducting prelistening speaking activities.

Discussion

See the General Teaching Tips, page 6, for suggestions on conducting discussions.

ANSWERS

* One woman is in her office. The other is in her car.
* Answers will vary.

Vocabulary Preview

See the General Teaching Tips, page 4, for suggestions on conducting the vocabulary preview.

B. LISTENING (page 9)

CULTURE NOTE

Ask students if they know what a "VP" is. Have students read the information in the box.

Main Ideas

See the General Teaching Tips, page 4, for suggestions on teaching the Main Ideas section.

❶ ANSWERS

Tara's good news	Shannon's reaction
She was offered the job of VP.	She's happy, excited for Tara.
Tara's bad news	Shannon's reaction
She's going to move to Atlanta.	She's surprised, disappointed, stunned.

Details and Inferences

See the General Teaching Tips, page 4, for suggestions on teaching this section.

❷ ANSWERS

1. c. Students can infer the answer because Shannon says she's on her way to work; also, she mentions traffic.
2. b
3. a
4. c

5. b
6. 1. a
   2. c
   3. d
   4. b

Listening for Language

See the General Teaching Tips, page 5, for suggestions on teaching this section.

CONVERSATION TOOLS

1. See the General Teaching Tips, page 6, for suggestions on teaching Conversation Tools.
2. Read aloud the expressions in the box. Be sure your voice conveys the proper emotion—happiness for good news, concern or sympathy for bad news.

❹ ANSWERS

I've got news; That's fabulous; That's (so) awesome; I don't know how to tell you this, but . . . ; I'm (just) stunned

1. See the General Teaching Tips, page 5, for suggestions on teaching Focus on Sound.
2. This book uses capital letters to indicate stressed words, lowercase letters for unstressed words, and italics. Capitalized words should not be exaggerated. These stressed words should be pronounced as described in the box.
3. Words that convey the essential meaning of the sentence are commonly called *content* words. *Function* words tend to express relationships among content words. A statement consisting only of content words would be "telegraphic"; it would be understood, though perhaps not perfectly. An utterance made up only of function words would be meaningless.
4. In Exercise 6, check that students stress the content words correctly.
5. In Exercise 7, some students may have trouble hearing the reduced words, as Tara speaks very quickly. If students need help, pause the recording after each item and have students repeat what they heard. Point out the reduced forms, if necessary.
6. In Exercise 7, some words are stressed more heavily than others. If students ask about this, tell them that they are hearing correctly and explain that speakers normally choose to emphasize some words more than others. Inform students that they will learn more about the "rules" of stress in subsequent chapters.

Expansion Activities to Train Students to Hear Stressed Words

- Select an audio passage, transcribe it, and replace the stressed words with blanks that students fill in as they listen. This helps students to both see and hear where the stressed words are.
- Dictate sentences and have students write down only the stressed words. Then have them reconstruct the full sentences using the stressed words as cues.
- Select another audio passage and transcribe it. Underline selected words in each sentence, some stressed and some unstressed. In class, play the audio sentence by sentence. Students must tell you whether each underlined word is stressed or not.

⑦ ANSWERS

1. Well, you know David and I have been talking about it . . .
2. Well it's not just a job, Shannon. It's my dream job.
3. I think I am going to have to take it.
4. It's so different, it's so far, I mean the food, the climate. . .
5. And I'd like to just, you know, try it for a couple of years because we can always move back.

C. REAL TALK: USE WHAT YOU'VE LEARNED (page 13)

Vocabulary Review

1. See the General Teaching Tips, page 6, for suggestions on conducting the vocabulary review.
2. Be sure to circulate as students are talking. Note cases where students both correctly and incorrectly use the vocabulary being reviewed.

Role Play

See the General Teaching Tips, page 7, for suggestions on conducting role plays.

Part Three: On the Air

Background

The recording is part of an interview with the authors of a book called *Mom, Can I Move Back In with You? A Survival Guide for Parents of Twenty-Somethings.* The book is about adult children who move back in with their parents after having lived on their own for a period of time.

Art

1. See the General Teaching Tips, page 3, for suggestions on presenting art.
2. Explain that "median" means *average*.
3. Have students make sentences about the information in the chart. If necessary, use questions to guide them. For example:
   * What information is provided in this chart? (Answer: Statistics for 1970 and 2003 on the median age of first marriage, the median age of women for first childbirth, and the percentage of young adults living with their parents.)
   * What has happened to the median age of first marriage since 1970? (Answer: It has increased for both men and women.)
   * At what age did the average woman have her first child in 1970? (Answer: 22.1) In 2003? (Answer: 24.8)

A. PRELISTENING (page 15)

See the General Teaching Tips, page 3, for suggestions on conducting prelistening speaking activities.

Discussion

See the General Teaching Tips, page 6, for suggestions on conducting discussions.

Vocabulary Preview

See the General Teaching Tips, page 4, for suggestions on conducting the vocabulary preview.

B. LISTENING (page 16)
Main Ideas

See the General Teaching Tips, page 4, for suggestions on teaching the Main Ideas section.

① ANSWERS

1. Biggest factor: economic

   Another factor: sociological ("It's taking longer for the emerging adult to really feel adult.")

2. longer than

3. responsible

4. No

Details and Inferences

See the General Teaching Tips, page 4, for suggestions on teaching this section.

② ANSWERS

1. b, d, e, f, g

2. b, c, d

3. c

4. a. A; b. I; c. I; d. A

5. b

6. a

Listening for Language

See the General Teaching Tips, page 5, for suggestions on teaching this section.

FOCUS ON SOUND

See the General Teaching Tips, page 5, for suggestions on teaching Focus on Sound.

④ ANSWERS

2. That seems like an excuse for bad parenting to me.

3. No, it's actually not an excuse for bad parenting.

4. . . . and they're coming out of college with at least twenty thousand dollars' worth of debt.

5. . . . and helping your child to become more adult is something you have to do

   with every one of your twenty somethings.

⑤ ANSWERS

Additional examples of linked or blended phrases from Audioscript page 237:

It's a question, parents are asking, between ages, move back in, emerging adult, big age of

23, have an apartment, a different time, coming out of college, get your act together or

move out

C. REAL TALK: USE WHAT YOU'VE LEARNED (page 19)

Vocabulary Review

1. See the General Teaching Tips, page 6, for suggestions on conducting the vocabulary review.
2. Be sure to circulate as students are talking. Note cases where students both correctly and incorrectly use the vocabulary being reviewed.

Role Play

See the General Teaching Tips, page 7, for suggestions on conducting role plays.

Part Four: In Class

Background

In this first chapter, spend some time talking to students about the importance and value of learning how to take notes. See the General Teaching Tips, Part Four, page 10.

Art

1. See the General Teaching Tips, page 3, for suggestions on presenting art.
2. Students may have seen other versions of the Cultural Adjustment Cycle. Some versions show five phases, others three. Different versions use different terms for the phases as well. However, the terms "honeymoon period" and "culture shock" are used widely.
3. The time spans given are approximations or averages. Each person experiences cultural adjustment differently.

A. PRELISTENING (page 21)

See the General Teaching Tips, page 10, for suggestions on conducting prelistening activities in this part of the chapter.

Discussion

See the General Teaching Tips, page 6, for suggestions on conducting discussions.

Vocabulary Preview

See the General Teaching Tips, page 4, for suggestions on conducting the vocabulary preview.

Pretest

Chapter 1 differs from the other chapters in this book in that this section begins with a pretest. The purpose is to provide both you and the student with baseline information about the student's ability to take notes. Have students refer back to these notes and evaluate them later, after they begin learning how to take efficient and well-organized notes.

① SUGGESTED PROCEDURE

1. Have students take out blank sheets of notebook paper.
2. Read the directions and check to be sure students understand what they are going to do. Reassure them that the purpose of this test is to find out what they already know about taking notes. The test will not be graded. Students should do their best, but they shouldn't worry if they don't understand everything.
3. Remind students that important words—key words—are stressed. They should listen for key words and write those in their notes.
4. Play the recording and observe as students take notes.
5. When the recording is finished, collect students' notes and hold them until the next class session.

② SUGGESTED PROCEDURE

1. Do not have students do this exercise on the same day as they do Exercise 1. Otherwise, they may be able to answer the questions from memory. The purpose of this exercise is for students to use their notes to answer the questions. This will give them and you an idea of how well they were able to take notes on their first attempt.
2. Redistribute students' notes from the previous lesson.
3. Read the directions and questions aloud. Have students write their answers to the questions on their own paper for you to collect.
4. Do not go over the answers at this time. Tell students they will hear the lecture again later and they will go over the answers to the questions at that time.

B. LISTENING AND NOTE-TAKING (page 23)

See the General Teaching Tips, page 10, for suggestions on teaching this section.

Lecture Organization and Language: Signposting

- From time to time in this book, Lecture Organization and Lecture Language are combined. See the General Teaching Tips, page 11, for suggestions on teaching these sections.
- In public speaking, *signposting* means telling listeners which topics a speaker plans to cover in a lecture or talk.

① SUGGESTED PROCEDURE

Have students read the information in the box silently, or call on various students to read the information aloud. Stop at the end of each section to ask if there are questions.

② SUGGESTED PROCEDURE

1. Read the directions.
2. Do item 1 as an example. Stop the recording after the item and check students' answers. Replay the item if necessary. Repeat this procedure as necessary for each item.

ANSWERS

Sentence	Announcement	Signal Transitions/ Signal Words	Question	What Speaker Will Talk About
1	✓			explain the process of culture shock
2			✓	define culture shock
3	✓			symptoms
4			✓	psychological factors
5		✓		summarize the lecture

Lecture Note Form: Tips for Writing Clear and Useful Notes

1. See the General Teaching Tips, page 11, for suggestions on teaching the Lecture Language section.
2. See Appendix 2, page 221 in the Student Book, for a list of common abbreviations and symbols.

❹ SUGGESTED PROCEDURE

Have students work in pairs. Have them look at the two sets of notes side by side, if possible, and note the similarities and differences.

❹ ANSWER

The notes in Example A are clearer and more useful because they are outlined consistently and indented correctly. Main ideas are underlined and each detail is numbered.

❺ PROCEDURE

This is a critically important step, so be sure to leave enough time for it.

1. Students can work alone or in pairs. If they work in pairs, have them exchange papers and give one another suggestions for ways to improve their notes.
2. Bring the class back together and call on students to report on the differences between their "before" and "after" notes.

❺ ANSWERS

Answers will vary and may include any of the tips from Exercise 3.

Taking Notes

See the General Teaching Tips, page 12, for suggestions on teaching this section.

⑥ SUGGESTED PROCEDURE

1. Students may add to their pretest notes or take new notes on a clean sheet of paper. The goal is for them to implement what they have learned about the characteristics of good notes.

2. Students may think they should take notes on the incomplete outline in the book. Do not allow them to do this. Explain the two-stage note-taking procedure that they will follow in this book and its rationale (see General Teaching Tips, Taking Notes, page 12). Students will always take notes on their own paper, then copy those notes onto the outline in the book. You may, however, allow students to look over the outline in the text before listening. Explain that the words in the margin on the left are cues to the content students need to listen for.

3. After listening, have students rewrite their notes in the book. Remind them to write key words only and to use abbreviations and symbols. *Note:* The cue words in the left margin do not replace the notes students need to write. For example, on the line where students see the cue "introduction/review," it is not enough for them to write those words. They must take notes on the *content* of the introduction. They must also remember to write a Roman numeral "I."

**introduction/
review**

Psych 10	March 14

CULTURE SHOCK

I. Intro / Review

    Cult. adjust. process:

        At first: euphoric period

        Stay longer: feel angry, upset, overreact = new stage

        = culture shock

II. Culture shock

    A. Def:

        1. Anxiety when rules we know don't work in new cult.

        2. Psych def: "Cognitive dissonance" = discomfort when

        new exper. don't match what we expect

    B. Symptoms

        1. Physical: headaches, overeating, sleep disord.

        2. Bizarre behav. or fears, cleanliness, shaking hands

        Ex: friend's son thought new country smelled funny

        3. Emotional = personality changes, e.g., anger,

        homesick, no confidence, lonely, depressed

(continued)

how to minimize symptoms (4 suggestions)	C. How to ↓ symptoms
	1. Understand cult. shock is normal
	2. Temporary; 3–6 mos.
	3. Be open-minded, flexible, curious, sense of humor
	4. Be self-aware
how to prepare for life in new culture (3 suggestions)	D. How to prepare for life in new cult.
	1. Read, talk to people, watch movies
	2. Learn lang.
	3. Dev. support system ahead of time = get names of people, orgs. that can help

Reviewing the Lecture

1. See the General Teaching Tips, page 13, for suggestions on conducting this activity.
2. *Optional:* Hand out the lecture script after students finish going over the pretest questions. See Using the Audioscript on page 14 of the General Teaching Tips.

⑧ ANSWERS

1. Culture shock is the feeling of anxiety that overtakes you when you realize that the rules that you thought you knew about how to get things done don't seem to work in the new culture.
2. Cognitive dissonance is the sense of discomfort that we feel when our new experiences don't match what we already know or expect.
3. Symptoms of culture shock:
   physical: headaches, overeating, sleep disorders
   mental (behavioral): worry about cleanliness, afraid to shake hands, complain that the air smells funny
   emotional: personality changes, irritation, anger, homesickness, loss of confidence, loneliness, depression, feel like another person is living in your body
4. People should recognize that culture shock is normal and temporary.
5. less likely: open-minded, flexible, curious, have a good sense of humor, self-aware, understand their own strengths and weaknesses
   more likely: rigid, judgmental
6. Before arriving in the new culture, try to learn as much about it as possible: read, talk to people, watch movies, try to learn a little bit of the language, develop a support system ahead of time.

C. REAL TALK: USE WHAT YOU'VE LEARNED (page 27)

See the General Teaching Tips, page 6, for suggestions on teaching this section.

Vocabulary Review

See the General Teaching Tips, page 6, for suggestions on conducting the vocabulary review.

Questionnaire: Factors Important to Successful Intercultural Adjustment

This activity presents personality factors that are conducive to successful intercultural adjustment. It provides students with language for describing people.

1. Follow the directions in the book.
2. At the end of the discussion, bring the whole class together and summarize students' ideas for ways to minimize culture shock.

TOEFL Practice

1. See the General Teaching Tips, page 14, for suggestions on conducting this activity.
2. Every student talk will be different, but a complete answer to the question will include both similarities and differences between culture shock and reverse culture shock.

❷ ANSWERS

Similarities:
Both processes are characterized by initial excitement, followed by a period of "shock" in which people experience alienation, irritability, hostility, and other uncomfortable symptoms.

Differences:
Culture shock is experienced when one goes to a new place. "Reverse" culture shock is felt when one returns home after a period of time away. Reverse shock is often more severe than culture shock because it is unexpected.

LEARNING A NEW LANGUAGE

Part One: In Person

Art

1. The photos show two types of learners: a "natural" learner, who is able to learn by interacting with speakers of the new language in informal settings, and a "formal" learner, who prefers learning in a classroom with a teacher. Most learners are a combination of these two types.
2. See the General Teaching Tips, page 3, for suggestions on presenting art.

A. PRELISTENING (page 30)

See the General Teaching Tips, page 3, for suggestions on conducting prelistening speaking activities.

Discussion

See the General Teaching Tips, page 6, for suggestions on conducting discussions.

Vocabulary Preview

See the General Teaching Tips, page 4, for suggestions on conducting the vocabulary preview.

B. LISTENING (page 31)
Main Ideas

See the General Teaching Tips, page 4, for suggestions on teaching the Main Ideas section.

🔘 ANSWERS

	Woman (Judy)	Man (Andrew)
Where they learned	U.S.	Japan
When they learned (age)	17	20s
Main factors in their success	motivation	Japanese girlfriend

Details and Inferences

See the General Teaching Tips, page 4, for suggestions on teaching this section.

❷ ANSWERS

1. a. B　b. A　c. J　d. A　e. B　f. A
2. a. J　b. B　c. A　d. A　e. J

Listening for Language

See the General Teaching Tips, page 5, for suggestions on teaching this section.

FOCUS ON SOUND

1. See the General Teaching Tips, page 5, for suggestions on teaching Focus on Sound.
2. If a speaker has finished a thought, the voice will rise slightly on the last stressed syllable of what is said. If the last stressed syllable is also the last syllable, the speaker's voice will *glide* down to its lowest pitch at the end. If the last stressed syllable is not the last syllable spoken, the speaker's voice will *drop* or *step* down to its lowest level.

❹ ANSWERS

2. rising	**6.** falling	**10.** rising
3. rising	**7.** rising	**11.** falling
4. falling	**8.** falling	
5. rising	**9.** rising	

CONVERSATION TOOLS

See the General Teaching Tips, page 6, for suggestions on teaching Conversation Tools.

❻ ANSWERS

Signals	Main Point
1. The point is	You can apply the new language in all aspects of daily life.
2. In other words, what I'm trying to get at is	A lot of people just use the language in one way, but they could use it more comprehensively.

C. REAL TALK: USE WHAT YOU'VE LEARNED (page 34)

Vocabulary Review

1. See the General Teaching Tips, page 6, for suggestions on conducting the vocabulary review.
2. Be sure to circulate as students are talking. Note cases where students both correctly and incorrectly use the vocabulary being reviewed.

❷ ANSWERS

1. motivation
2. rehearse
3. flash cards
4. immigrant
5. fit in with her peers

6. pick up
7. comprehensively
8. easier said than done
9. in the habit of

Find Someone Who . . .

1. Read aloud the directions in the book. Explain to students that they should circulate among their classmates and ask questions using the prompts in the chart. They should talk to each person only until that person answers "yes" to a question and write that person's name in the blank. They should then move on to speak with someone else. They should not write any person's name more than once.
2. You may wish to give a time limit and encourage students to record as many names as they can in the time allotted.

Discussion

See the General Teaching Tips, page 6, for suggestions on conducting discussions.

Part Two: On the Phone

Art

The art consists of brochures from two English-language schools, the American Language Institute and the English Language Center. See the General Teaching Tips, page 3, for suggestions on presenting art.

A. PRELISTENING (page 37)

See the General Teaching Tips, page 3, for suggestions on conducting prelistening speaking activities.

Discussion

See the General Teaching Tips, page 6, for suggestions on conducting discussions.

Vocabulary Preview

See the General Teaching Tips, page 4, for suggestions on conducting the vocabulary preview.

B. LISTENING (page 38)

CULTURE NOTE

Ask students if they have ever called an English-speaking business. Ask what kinds of phrases were used by the person who answered the phone. In addition to those in the Culture Note, some other phrases commonly used are "How may I direct your call?" or simply "This is (name), may I help you?"

Main Ideas

1. See the General Teaching Tips, page 4, for suggestions on teaching the Main Ideas section.
2. *Optional:* If it is not possible to have students work in small groups for this activity, have the whole class listen to both phone calls and compare answers to the exercises.

❶ ANSWERS

ELC

1. English Language Center
2. to get information for her nephew
3. February 5th
4. three

ALI

1. American Language Institute
2. to get information for her nephew
3. February 5th
4. two

Details and Inferences

See the General Teaching Tips, page 4, for suggestions on teaching this section.

❷ ANSWERS

	English Language Center			American Language Institute	
Program	1	2	3	1	2
Type	intensive	semi-intensive	half-day	intensive (academic purposes)	intensive (everyday communication)
Hours per week	30	24	20	23	20
Schedule	full-time	no afternoon classes on Monday or Friday	no afternoon classes	9-3 Monday-Thursday 9-12 Friday	9-3 Monday-Thursday No classes Friday
Course length	4 weeks	4 weeks	4 weeks	10 weeks	4 weeks
Cost	$1,150	$995	$895	$2,750	$1,400
Types of classes	all skills		no electives		listening and speaking + emphasis like business or tourism
Class size	12 max, 8-9 average	12 max, 8-9 average	12 max, 8-9 average		18 max (summer) 14 now

❸ ANSWERS

ELC semi-intensive or ALI Program 2. These programs are best for his schedule and his job needs.

Listening for Language

See the General Teaching Tips, page 5, for suggestions on teaching this section.

FOCUS ON SOUND

1. See the General Teaching Tips, page 5, for suggestions on teaching Focus on Sound.
2. Students may notice that within thought groups, one word is stressed more strongly than others. Remind them that there are several "levels" of stress (see note in Chapter 1, Focus on Sound, page 22, item 6 of this Teacher's Manual) and inform students that they will learn more about stress in Chapter 2 Focus on Sound, page 45 of (the Student Book).
3. After listening, have students practice reading the sentences in pairs.

❺ ANSWERS

2. We have an <u>intensive</u> <u>English</u> <u>program</u>, / which is our most <u>comprehensive</u>.
3. That covers a <u>grammar</u> class, / and a <u>conversation</u> and <u>listening</u> <u>skills</u> <u>class</u>, / <u>and</u> a <u>reading</u> and <u>writing</u> <u>class</u> / in the <u>afternoon</u>.
4. And the <u>cost</u> for <u>that</u> / is <u>eleven</u> <u>hundred</u> and <u>fifty</u> <u>dollars</u> / for a <u>four-week</u> <u>session</u>.
5. The <u>third</u> <u>option</u> / is the <u>half-day</u> <u>program</u>, / and <u>that's</u> <u>twenty</u> <u>lessons</u> per <u>week</u>. / <u>This one</u>, / there's <u>no</u> <u>classes</u> at <u>all</u> in the <u>afternoon</u>. / It's <u>eight hundred</u> and <u>ninety-five dollars</u> for the <u>four-week</u> <u>session</u>, / <u>students</u> are in <u>class</u> from <u>nine</u> in the <u>morning</u> / till <u>twelve forty-five</u>, / and then they're <u>free</u> / in the <u>afternoon</u>.
6. **Caller**: Um, and did <u>you</u> <u>say</u> / this <u>program</u> was <u>twenty</u> <u>hours</u> a <u>week</u>?
   School Employee: Yes, <u>twenty</u> <u>hours</u>, / it's <u>Monday</u> through <u>Thursday</u> / from <u>nine</u> to <u>three</u> / with no classes on <u>Friday</u>.

CONVERSATION TOOLS

See the General Teaching Tips, page 6, for suggestions on teaching Conversation Tools.

❼ ANSWERS

CALL 1

1. meaning   2. do you mean

CALL 2

3. meaning   4. you said   5. did you say

C. REAL TALK: USE WHAT YOU'VE LEARNED (page 41)

Vocabulary Review

1. See the General Teaching Tips, page 6, for suggestions on conducting the vocabulary review.
2. Be sure to circulate as students are talking. Note cases where students both correctly and incorrectly use the vocabulary being reviewed.

Role Play

1. See the General Teaching Tips, page 7, for suggestions on conducting role plays.
2. *Optional:* Students can substitute the information given here for the information in the audioscript. They can then use the audioscript as the basis for their role plays.

STUDENT A: AMERICAN LANGUAGE INSTITUTE

Dates and days: Option 1: 1/12–2/6, Monday and Wednesday
Option 2: 2/22–3/22, Tuesday and Thursday

Times: 6:30–9:00	**Cost:** $430
Hours per week: 5	**Course name:** Advanced
Number of meetings: 10	**Class size:** Maximum of 12

STUDENT B: ENGLISH LANGUAGE CENTER

Dates and days: 1/3–1/31; 2/7–2/28
Monday and Wednesday or Tuesday and Thursday

Times: 6:30–9:00	**Cost:** $350
Hours per week: 5	**Course name:** Intermediate/Advanced
Number of meetings: 8	**Class size:** Maximum of 10

Part Three: On the Air

Background

"Think different" was the advertising slogan for Apple Computers in the late 1990s. It was featured on posters and billboards that showed famous people including Bob Dylan, as seen here, as well as Albert Einstein, Pablo Picasso, Mahatma Gandhi, John Lennon and Yoko Ono, and others. "Think different" is ungrammatical; it should be "Think differently." This error is the topic of the listening.

Art

1. The famous person in the billboard is Bob Dylan. The slogan "Think different" is meant to encourage people to be original like Dylan, an American singer, songwriter, musician, and poet who has been a major figure in popular music since the 1960s.
2. See the General Teaching Tips, page 3, for suggestions on presenting art.

A. PRELISTENING (page 43)
Discussion

See the General Teaching Tips, page 6, for suggestions on conducting discussions.

Vocabulary Preview

See the General Teaching Tips, page 4, for suggestions on conducting the vocabulary preview.

B. LISTENING (page 43)

Main Ideas

See the General Teaching Tips, page 4, for suggestions on teaching the Main Ideas section.

❶ ANSWERS

    1. using adjectives instead of *-ly* adverbs in expressions such as "fresh-baked bread"
    2. c

Details and Inferences

See the General Teaching Tips, page 4, for suggestions on teaching this section.

❷ ANSWERS

    1. a. fresh-baked bread; b. think smart   **3.** b
    2. c   **4.** Yes: fresh-baked bread, Go slow, fresh-cut flowers
    No: He speaks real good.

❸ ANSWERS

    1. d   **2.** f   **3.** b   **4.** a   **5.** c   **6.** e

Listening for Language

See the General Teaching Tips, page 5, for suggestions on teaching this section.

FOCUS ON SOUND

    1. See the General Teaching Tips, page 5, for suggestions on teaching Focus on Sound.
    2. Do not expect students to be able to absorb all these guidelines at one sitting. Your goal at this stage should be to help students build an awareness of native stress patterns. Point out the examples of the guidelines presented here, but do not expect students to be able to follow all of them yet.

❺ ANSWERS

    1. wonder, happened, freshly   **4.** Korva, I, slow, slowly
    2. Apple, Think, different   **5.** go, fresh, freshly
    3. little, fence   **6.** agree, adverb, siege

C. REAL TALK: USE WHAT YOU'VE LEARNED (page 46)

Vocabulary Review

    1. See the General Teaching Tips, page 6, for suggestions on conducting the vocabulary review.
    2. Be sure to circulate as students are talking. Note cases where students both correctly and incorrectly use the vocabulary being reviewed.

❷ Answers

1. pet peeve **3.** has an ear for **5.** endangered species **7.** idiomatic

2. under siege **4.** on the fence **6.** violations

Survey

1. See the General Teaching Tips, page 8, for suggestions on conducting interviews and surveys.
2. If students do not have access to native speakers of English outside of class, have them interview you, other teachers in your school, or people who speak English well (even if they are not natives). If there are no speakers of English available, have students conduct a modified survey on the Internet. Using a search engine such as Google, have them type in the phrases in the survey and simply see how many "hits" come up for each phrase. For example, the phrase "newborn baby" yields more than 2.5 million hits, whereas "newly born baby" yields fewer than 50,000. Remind students to use quotation marks when they type the phrases into the search engine.

Part Four: In Class

Art

1. The cartoon *Zits* has been very popular in North America for quite a few years. It features a teenage boy named Jeremy, his parents, and his friends. In this particular scene, in addition to "über," Jeremy uses the word "supersize," which refers to extremely large portions of fast food sold at chains like McDonald's. "Totally" is an expression that has been used commonly by North American teenagers.
2. See the General Teaching Tips, page 3, for suggestions on presenting art.

A. PRELISTENING (page 48)

See the General Teaching Tips, page 10, for suggestions on conducting prelistening activities in this part of the chapter.

Quiz

The purpose of this quiz is to provide students with some background about the history of the English language. It should not be graded.

Answers

1. c
2. d. The count of the number of words in English depends on whether one counts only roots or also derivative forms, such as "turn, turns, turned, turning," etc. Furthermore, if a word has multiple meanings, the count would depend on either counting each meaning separately or counting all of them as one. No one knows exactly how many words English has, but many people estimate that the number is close to one million.

(*continued*)

3. b. German is the "mother" of a group of European languages that includes English, Dutch, Swedish, Norwegian, and Danish.

4. a

5. c. Latin is the mother language of French (also Spanish, Italian, Portuguese, and others). Though some words were also transformed from Latin to German and later to English, most Latin-based words came into English as a result of the Norman Conquest of Britain in the year 1066. Because of this French victory, many French-speaking people emigrated to Britain.

6. a. A compound noun consists of two nouns that are combined to form a new word.

7. d. The sandwich is named after an eighteenth-century English nobleman, the Earl of Sandwich.

8. b. The root of a word is the part to which prefixes and suffixes are attached. "Caff" is also the root of the word "coffee."

Vocabulary Preview

See the General Teaching Tips, page 4, for suggestions on conducting the vocabulary preview.

Discussion

See the General Teaching Tips, page 6, for suggestions on conducting discussions.

B. LISTENING AND NOTE-TAKING (page 51)

See the General Teaching Tips, page 10, for suggestions on teaching this section.

Lecture Language: Cohesion

1. See the General Teaching Tips, page 11, for suggestions on teaching Lecture Language.

2. The cohesive devices listed here are also used in writing. As a preliminary activity, you may want to select another written piece and use it to provide examples of these devices before students hear them in the lecture.

🎧 ANSWERS

1. Cohesive devices:

Sample 1: repetition of key word root; use of words from the same "family" (root, language, nouns, verbs, consonants, vowels); reference

Sample 2: unity; repetition of key words (language, German, Germanic, English); use of synonyms (language, tongue; later, eventually; similarities, almost all, almost the same, the same); use of words from the same "family" (language, tongue, linguists; German, English, Swedish, Danish, other European languages; grammar, vocabulary, definite/indefinite articles, words, pronounced); reference (the time, this language, The proof of this, those other languages, they all have, they're almost the same); transitions (And, In other words, For example, Also, Or)

2. **Sample 2** is more cohesive because it has unity; it is clearly about one topic. It has many more words from the same family, and it also uses more transitions.

Answers

Technique(s): processes, way, processes
Coin: creating, formed, acquires

❹ **Answers**

1. f   **2.** b   **3.** d   **4.** d

Lecture Note Form: Graphic Lecture Notes

1. See the General Teaching Tips, page 11, for suggestions on teaching this section.
2. *Nonlinear* or *graphic notes* are not written in outline form. Instead, they employ diagrams, maps, or other visuals as the framework for note-taking. For more information about such frameworks, do an Internet search for "graphic organizers."

❻ **Answers**

1. sources of borrowed English words
2. four (Old German, Latin, French, and proper names)
3. the percentage of words from each source, the types of words, how they came into English, and examples of borrowed words

Taking Notes

1. See the General Teaching Tips, page 12, for suggestions on teaching this section.
2. Follow the directions in the book precisely. Students should copy the concept map and take notes on their own paper. They should then edit and rewrite their notes in the book.

❼ **Sample Outline**

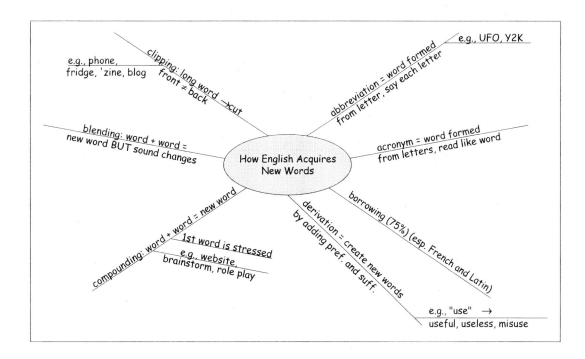

Reviewing the Lecture

See the General Teaching Tips, page 13, for suggestions on conducting this activity.

⑧ ANSWERS

  1. We mean that English acquires these words through contact with other languages, such as French and German.

  2. See the Sample Outline under Taking Notes on page 41.

  3. They have different stresses: "RACE car" and "CAR race." The former is a kind of car. The latter is a kind of race.

C. REAL TALK: USE WHAT YOU'VE LEARNED (page 55)

See the General Teaching Tips, page 6, for suggestions on teaching this section.

Vocabulary Review

See the General Teaching Tips, pages 6, for suggestions on conducting the vocabulary review.

Word Creation Game

All of the blended words are "real" and appear in numerous dictionaries. Some, such as "chocoholic," are used only colloquially. Others can be used formally as well.

ANSWERS

1. brainiac	**3.** travelogue	**5.** brunch	**7.** spyware
2. chocoholic	**4.** rockumentary	**6.** biohazard	

TOEFL Practice

  1. See the General Teaching Tips, page 14, for suggestions on conducting this activity.

  2. Every student talk will be different. In a typical presentation, the speaker may begin by saying that English is a language that borrows extensively from other languages, that there are six processes by which foreign words become part of the English language, and that *podcasting* and *broadcast* are examples of two of these processes: blending and compound nouns, respectively. Each speaker should define or explain each of these processes with examples.

CHAPTER 3   IN THE MONEY

Part One: In Person

Background

If a person is *in the money,* it means the person has a lot of money. Other idiomatic expressions for talking about money are presented throughout this chapter.

Art

1. The photos show ways that people can save money, e.g., shopping at store sales and at garage sales.
2. See the General Teaching Tips, page 3, for suggestions on presenting art.

A. PRELISTENING (page 59)

See the General Teaching Tips, page 3, for suggestions on conducting prelistening speaking activities.

Discussion

See the General Teaching Tips, page 6, for suggestions on conducting discussions.

Vocabulary Preview

See the General Teaching Tips, page 4, for suggestions on conducting the vocabulary preview.

B. LISTENING (page 60)

Main Ideas

See the General Teaching Tips, page 4, for suggestions on teaching the Main Ideas section.

🕐 ANSWERS

Answers will vary but should include at least ten of the following:

live within one's means	don't overspend on credit cards
sew one's own clothes	go to garage sales
buy clothes on sale	bring lunch to work from home
don't eat in restaurants	take the bus or walk
never spend more than you have coming in	don't go grocery shopping when you're hungry
follow a budget	use coupons
don't borrow	always ask for a discount
put money into a retirement plan	

Details and Inferences

See the General Teaching Tips, page 4, for suggestions on teaching this section.

② ANSWERS

1. F. She was working part-time.

2. F. The daughter wanted a cashmere sweater, but she didn't get one.

3. T

4. T

5. F. She has no credit card debt.

6. T

7. T

Listening for Language

See the General Teaching Tips, page 5, for suggestions on teaching this section.

CONVERSATION TOOLS

See the General Teaching Tips, page 6, for suggestions on teaching Conversation Tools.

④ ANSWERS

1. make ends meet

2. live within your means

3. stick to a budget

4. Itemize

5. cut down on

6. cut corners

7. doing without

⑤ ANSWERS

1. e	**3.** b	**5.** f	**7.** c
2. b	**4.** a	**6.** d	

FOCUS ON SOUND

1. See the General Teaching Tips, page 5, for suggestions on teaching Focus on Sound.

2. Some question types may be unfamiliar to students. It is helpful to provide a context for them. For example, echo questions are always a response to something someone said previously, for example:

A: I'm living on a strict budget right now.

B: A budget?

3. The two types of tag questions powerfully illustrate the importance of intonation in English. Using incorrect intonation in the tag will send a very misleading message. Demonstrate and make sure students can hear and understand the difference between the two types of tags.

⑧ ANSWERS
Set 1

1. How often do you go shopping for GROceries?

2. You're taking HOW many classes this (quarter/semester/year)?

3. That's a very expensive REStaurant, ISn't it?

4. Have you heard any news from HOME?

5. Who's that GUY over there?

Set 2

1. Have you ever borrowed money from a FRIEND

2. You don't have any CREDit cards, DO YOU?

3. Do you DRIVE to school, or do you WALK?

4. When do you want to go SHOPping?

5. You spent HOW MUCH MONEY on FOOD last WEEK?

C. REAL TALK: USE WHAT YOU'VE LEARNED (page 64)

Vocabulary Review

1. See the General Teaching Tips, page 6, for suggestions on conducting the vocabulary review.
2. Be sure to circulate as students are talking. Note cases where students both correctly and incorrectly use the vocabulary being reviewed.

❷ SAMPLE ANSWERS

Questions will vary. For example:

Have you ever owned a brand-new car?
Do you use coupons to save money at the supermarket?
What are some good ways to cut corners?
What are some extras that you could do without if you had to cut corners?
Do you ever shop at garage sales?
Do you worry about being in debt?
Do you itemize your expenses each month?
What's the best way to make ends meet?
Is it hard for you to stick to a budget / live within your means?
How much interest do you pay each month on credit cards?

Role Play

See the General Teaching Tips, page 7, for suggestions on conducting role plays.

Part Two: On the Phone

Art

1. The photos show the two speakers in the recording: a female bank clerk and a male student from India.
2. See the General Teaching Tips, page 3, for suggestions on presenting art.

A. PRELISTENING (page 66)

See the General Teaching Tips, page 3, for suggestions on conducting prelistening speaking activities.

Discussion

1. See the General Teaching Tips, page 6, for suggestions on conducting discussions.
2. *Optional:* Start the lesson by asking students to raise their hands if they have a bank account. Then ask what type of accounts they have. As students speak, write topic-related vocabulary on the board.

Vocabulary Preview

See the General Teaching Tips, page 4, for suggestions on conducting the vocabulary preview.

B. LISTENING (page 66)

Main Ideas

See the General Teaching Tips, page 4, for suggestions on teaching the Main Ideas section.

❶ ANSWERS
   1. a, b   **2.** two, one   **3.** c

Details and Inferences

See the General Teaching Tips, page 4, for suggestions on teaching this section.

❷ ANSWERS
   1. Yes: a, c, e
      No: b, d
   2. c

3.

Account Type	Opening Balance	Service Charge (Fee)	Minimum Balance to Avoid Service Charge	Interest Rate
Basic savings	$100	$3 (if balance falls below $300)	$300	0.4%
Checking	$1	$12 for checks $0 monthly		
Basic money market	$1,000	$10 (if balance falls below $2,500)	$2,500	0.5%

4. d

5. b

6. c

7. He will probably open a basic savings account and a linked checking account. He could open a money market account, but it requires a minimum balance of $2,500 and the caller has only $5,400. He wouldn't have much money available to spend if he opened the money market account.

Listening for Language

See the General Teaching Tips, page 5, for suggestions on teaching this section.

CONVERSATION TOOLS

See the General Teaching Tips, page 6, for suggestions on teaching Conversation Tools.

❹ ANSWERS

1. a. minimum balance; b. service charge; c. balance; d. debit card; e. ATM card
2. a. service charge; b. waived; c. linked account; d. checking account
3. automatic transfer
4. a. interest rate; b. savings account
5. a. money market; b. opening balance
6. credit card

FOCUS ON SOUND

1. See the General Teaching Tips, page 5, for suggestions on teaching Focus on Sound.
2. If you are not a native speaker and you are not sure whether a phrase is a compound noun or an adjective + noun phrase, check a dictionary. Noun compounds are usually listed; adjective + noun phrases are not.

❻ Answers

1. a. MÍNimum BÁLance, b. SÉRVice charge, c. BÁLance, d. DÉBit card, e. atM card

2. a. SÉRvice charge, b. waived, c. LÍNKED account, d. CHÉCKing account

3. autoMÁTic TRÁNSfer

4. a. ÍNterest rate, b. SÁVings account

5. a. MÓNey market, b. Ópening BÁLance

6. CRÉDit card

C. REAL TALK: USE WHAT YOU'VE LEARNED (page 70)

Vocabulary Review

1. See the General Teaching Tips page 6, for suggestions on conducting the vocabulary review.
2. Be sure to circulate as students are talking. Note cases where students both correctly and incorrectly use the vocabulary being reviewed.

❷ Sample Answers

Questions will vary. For example:
Can I get an ATM card if I have a checking account at your bank?
Do you have automatic transfer from checking to savings?
Can I use a credit card for ID?
Do you offer a debit card?
What is the interest rate on the money market account?
Do you have a checking account that's linked to savings?
What's the minimum balance in a regular savings account?
What's the opening balance for a money market account?
How many kinds of savings accounts do you offer?
Is there a service charge on the checking account?
If I have a savings account, do you waive the fee on the checking account?

Role Play

1. See the General Teaching Tips page 7, for suggestions on conducting role plays.
2. Students who are not in an English-speaking country can get information on bank accounts by using the Internet. Using a search engine, have students type in the name of a bank, such as "Bank of America," "HSBC," or "Wells Fargo," and read the information on the website about bank accounts.

Part Three: On the Air

Art

1. The photo shows people handling American one- and five-dollar bills.
2. See the General Teaching Tips page 3, for suggestions on presenting art.

A. PRELISTENING (page 72)

See the General Teaching Tips, page 3, for suggestions on conducting prelistening speaking activities.

Discussion

1. See the General Teaching Tips, page 6, for suggestions on conducting discussions.
2. The Shakespeare quote can be paraphrased as "Do not borrow or lend money. If you borrow money, you are likely to lose both the money and the friend you borrowed it from."
3. *Borrow* and *lend* are transitive verbs: People borrow something from someone; they lend something to someone. *Loan* can be a verb or a noun. As a verb, it is used like *lend*.

Vocabulary Preview

See the General Teaching Tips, page 4, for suggestions on conducting the vocabulary preview.

B. LISTENING (page 73)

CULTURE NOTE

The explanation of "small claims court" is offered here because the speaker, Michelle Singletary, mentions it.

Main Ideas

See the General Teaching Tips, page 4, for suggestions on teaching the Main Ideas section.

❶ ANSWERS
1. Don't lend money that you need back.
2. She asks what they need the money for.
3. make a contract
4. to lend money to people in their family

Details and Inferences

See the General Teaching Tips, page 4, for suggestions on teaching this section.

❷ ANSWERS

Segment 1: c
Segment 2: b
Segment 3: a, b, d
Segment 4: a. how much they're borrowing; b. when you expect the money back
Segment 5: c
Segment 6: a

Listening for Language

See the General Teaching Tips, page 5, for suggestions on teaching this section.

FOCUS ON SOUND

1. See the General Teaching Tips, page 5, for suggestions on teaching Focus on Sound.
2. As students do Exercise 4, circulate and monitor them for correct stress and linking.

CONVERSATION TOOLS

See the General Teaching Tips, page 6, for suggestions on teaching Conversation Tools.

⑥ ANSWERS

cut BACK, cut DOWN on, cut OUT, do withOUT, get BY, pay BACK, pay OFF

C. REAL TALK: USE WHAT YOU'VE LEARNED (page 77)

Vocabulary Review

1. See the General Teaching Tips, page 6, for suggestions on conducting the vocabulary review.
2. See Chapter 2, Part One, page 34, for instructions on conducting Find Someone Who . . . activities.

Discussion

See the General Teaching Tips, page 6, for suggestions on conducting discussions.

Role Play

See the General Teaching Tips, page 7, for suggestions on conducting role plays.

Part Four: In Class

Background

The credit card facts here are from the year 2004. You can find updated statistics by going to the sources provided.

Art

See the General Teaching Tips, page 3, for suggestions on presenting art.

A. PRELISTENING (page 79)

See the General Teaching Tips, page 10, for suggestions on conducting prelistening speaking activities in this part of the chapter.

Discussion

See the General Teaching Tips, page 6, for suggestions on conducting discussions.

Vocabulary Preview

See the General Teaching Tips, page 4, for suggestions on conducting the vocabulary preview.

B. LISTENING AND NOTE-TAKING (page 80)

See the General Teaching Tips, page 10, for suggestions on teaching this section.

Lecture Note Form: Taking Notes on Numbers and Statistics

See the General Teaching Tips, page 11, for suggestions on teaching this section.

➋ ANSWERS

2. U.S savings rate:
   1993: 5.9%
   2003: 1.3%
3. 2002 av. salary:
   males: $35,487
   females: $30,093
4. Av. fee for late cred. card payment:
   2004: $39
   1996: $10

Lecture Language: Expressions for *Increase* and *Decrease*

1. See the General Teaching Tips, page 11, for suggestions on teaching Lecture Language.
2. Take some time to go over the synonyms. Provide additional examples, and try to elicit examples from the students.

➍ SAMPLE ANSWERS

1. 1992–2001, av. cred. card debt ↑ by 55% to $4,008 per household
2. @ same time, bankruptcy rate ↑ by 19%
3. 70% had cred. cards in 2001
4. 2003 unemp. rate = 10%
5. 1992: 42% of sts. borrowed $ for college; grad. w/ av. debt of $9,000
6. 2002: 66% "   "   "   "   "   "   ;   "   "   " debt = $18,900

Taking Notes

1. See the General Teaching Tips, page 12, for suggestions on teaching this section.
2. In Exercise 6, have students examine the Sample Budget for Recent College Graduate. Ask them which expenses they also have, how much they spend on the items listed, and/or how much money they usually have left at the end of the month.
3. In Exercise 7, follow the directions in the book precisely. Students should take notes on their own paper. They should then edit and rewrite their notes in the book.

description ◯	I. Intro
	Topic: Credit card debt @ college grads, 25–34
	Recent coll. grads:
	1st or 2nd job
	maybe newly married
	starting to have kids
	have more debt than any gen. in U.S. history
facts	II. Facts
year	• 1992–2001:
	av. cred. card debt ↑ 55%, = $4,008 per household
	bankruptcy rate ↑ 19%
year	• 2001:
	70% had credit cards
	71% had revolv. balance (= make monthly payment)
definition ◯	• Revolv. balance = make monthly payment, interest
	each month → debt increases
central question	III. Central question: Why is this gen. going into debt?
reasons	1. High cost of housing, transp., child care, etc.
	2. Weak labor market
	Large % of college grads have temp or pt-time jobs.
	2003: unemp. rate of 10%
	3. ↑ student loan debt
past	Past: Sts. used scholarships & grants to pay for
	coll. (don't need to pay back)
present	Present: This gen. pays w/ loans

loan stats ◯

yr.	% borrowed	av. debt at grad.
1992	42%	$9,000
2002	66%	$18,900

result	Diff. financial situation
example	Ex: Typical coll. grad "Caroline"
	Earns $36,000 / yr.
	Takes home $2,058/mo.
	Debt: $182 / mo. for loans, $125 for cred. cards
	Doesn't spend on lux.
	If unexpected expense?→Use cred. card = more debt
4th reason (2 parts)	4. Easy to get credit + poor money manage. skills

Reviewing the Lecture

See the General Teaching Tips, page 13, for suggestions on conducting this activity.

C. REAL TALK: USE WHAT YOU'VE LEARNED (page 86)

See the General Teaching Tips, page 6, for suggestions on teaching this section.

Vocabulary Review

See the General Teaching Tips, pages 6, for suggestions on conducting the vocabulary review.

ANSWERS

1. labor market
2. plastic
3. revolving balance
4. students loans, grants
5. bankruptcy

6. segment
7. accumulate
8. impact
9. going broke
10. doubled

Discussion

See the General Teaching Tips, page 6, for suggestions on conducting discussions.

Practice with Statistics

ANSWERS

Answers will vary.

Student A's sentences

1. In 1998, South Koreans made a total of $53 billion worth of purchases using credit cards. By 2002, this amount had increased to $519 billion.
2. In 1993, the U.S. personal savings rate was 5.9 percent. Ten years later, in 2003, it had declined to 1.3 percent.

3. In 1999, only 53,300 Americans paid their taxes by credit card. By 2003, this number had increased to 313,000.

4. The average cost of tuition at a U.S. public university was $9,338 in 2002. It was $10,818 in 2005.

Notes on Student B's sentences

1. In France:

       39 million debit cards

       9 million cred. cards

2. Av. cost of tuition at priv. U.S. univ.

       2002: $24,851

       2005: $28,769

3. U.S. fast-food purchases made by cred. card:

       2002: $6.1 billion

       2003: $12.9 billion

4. U.S. revolving debt:

    Jan. 1994: $313 billion

    Jan. 2004: $753 billion

❷ ANSWERS

Student B's sentences

1. In 2004, there were 39 million debit cards in France. By contrast, there were only 9 million credit cards.

2. The average cost of tuition at a private U.S. university was $24,851 in 2002. By 2005 it had risen to $28,769.

3. In 2002, Americans made $6.1 billion worth of fast-food purchases with credit cards. In 2003 the amount doubled to $12.9 billion.

4. In January of 1994, the U.S. had $313 billion in revolving debt. Ten years later, the amount was $753 billion.

Notes on Student A's sentences

1. Purchases w/ credit cards, S. Korea:

       1998: $53 billion

       2002: $519 billion

2. U.S. personal svgs. rate:

       1993: 5.9%

       2003: 1.3%

3. Americans who paid taxes by cred. card:

       1999: 53,300

       2003: 313,000

4. Av. tuition at U.S. public university:

       2002: $9,338

       2005: $10,818

TOEFL Practice

See the General Teaching Tips, page 14, for suggestions on conducting this activity.

⚙ SAMPLE ANSWERS

Every student talk will be different, but a complete presentation should include the following information:

Advantages of owning credit cards
Credit cards are helpful for:
* establishing credit
* having money available for emergencies
* travel arrangements
* shopping by phone or Internet
* conducting cashless transactions

Disadvantages of owning credit cards
Irresponsible or inexperienced young people face the danger of accumulating credit card debt due to poor money-management skills, revolving balance, and high interest rates on credit cards.

Part One: In Person

Background

This section is about sensory memories, that is, memories that are triggered by the senses of sight, sound, taste, smell, and touch.

Art

1. The photo shows a woman looking at a bouquet of flowers and having a pleasant memory.
2. See the General Teaching Tips, page 3, for suggestions on presenting art.

A. PRELISTENING (page 90)

See the General Teaching Tips, page 3, for suggestions on conducting prelistening speaking activities.

Discussion

1. See the General Teaching Tips, page 6, for suggestions on conducting discussions.
2. Explain what a *trigger* is: the part of a gun that, when pressed with one's finger, causes the gun to fire. This word is used figuratively here, with the meaning of "cause" or "stimulate."

Vocabulary Preview

See the General Teaching Tips, page 4, for suggestions on conducting the vocabulary preview.

B. LISTENING (page 91)
Main Ideas

See the General Teaching Tips, page 4, for suggestions on teaching the Main Ideas section.

❶ ANSWERS

Segment	Sense	Memory
1	smell	Speaker 1: sawdust Speaker 2: pipe tobacco
2	taste	fish
3	sight	colors—purple and green
4	feel, smell	a baseball

Details and Inferences

See the General Teaching Tips, page 4, for suggestions on teaching this section.

② ANSWERS

SEGMENT 1
1. T   **2.** U   **3.** U

SEGMENT 2
4. U   **5.** T

SEGMENT 3
6. F. She says they are not colors that she wears often.   **7.** T

SEGMENT 4
8. T   **9.** U   **10.** T

Listening for Language

See the General Teaching Tips, page 5, for suggestions on teaching this section.

FOCUS ON SOUND

See the General Teaching Tips, page 5, for suggestions on teaching Focus on Sound.

④ ANSWERS

2. Joe should call, not e-mail.
3. Mark, not Hannah, will bring the coffee.
4. Both women have doctors' appointments. Lynn's is today, while Cathy's is tomorrow.
5. The table and chair go in different locations.

⑤ PROCEDURE

1. Students probably have never done an exercise like this, so be sure to explain that on the recording they will hear *answers* to the questions in the book. Take time to go over the example and make sure that students understand the procedure.
2. Have students read all the questions before you play the recording.
3. Tell students to listen carefully for the word with the strongest stress in each answer. They will use this information to match the answers with the questions.

⑥ ANSWERS

a. 2   b. 4   c. 3   d. 5   e. 1

C. REAL TALK: USE WHAT YOU'VE LEARNED (page 93)

Vocabulary Review

See the General Teaching Tips, page 6, for suggestions on conducting the vocabulary review.

ANSWERS

 1. brings back / triggers   **3.** reminds me

 2. evocative   **4.** transports / take me back

Describing Memories

 1. Model the example in the book with a student.
 2. *Optional:* Model another example with a student partner. Have the student describe one of his or her sense memories. Respond with contrastive stress.

Part Two: On the Phone

Art

 1. The photo shows a man speaking on the phone at home.
 2. See the General Teaching Tips, page 3, for suggestions on presenting art.

A. PRELISTENING (page 94)

See the General Teaching Tips, page 3, for suggestions on conducting prelistening speaking activities.

Discussion

See the General Teaching Tips, page 6, for suggestions on conducting discussions.

Vocabulary Preview

See the General Teaching Tips, page 4, for suggestions on conducting the vocabulary preview.

B. LISTENING (page 95)
Main Ideas

See the General Teaching Tips, page 4, for suggestions on teaching the Main Ideas section.

ANSWERS

 1. The wife is upset because her husband forgot to call her.
 2. He says he has a thousand things on his mind.
 3. He plans to start writing things down.
 4. They are no longer angry. Their voices are calm, and the wife makes a joke.

Details and Inferences

See the General Teaching Tips, page 4, for suggestions on teaching this section.

ANSWERS

 1. a. N   b. H   c. W   d. H   e. N

2. b. She says she's on her way to pick up Joseph.

d. He says he'd better start writing things down.

e. The husband says he's got a thousand things on his mind, too.

Listening for Language

See the General Teaching Tips, page 5, for suggestions on teaching this section.

FOCUS ON SOUND

See the General Teaching Tips, page 5, for suggestions on teaching Focus on Sound.

4 ANSWERS

Strong emotion:

Wife: Howard! I can't believe you did this again!

Husband: Now hold on. Look who's talking.

Wife: Yeah, I've been telling you to do that!

Husband: Yeah, I know. I apologize.

Calming down:

Wife: We've got to do something about this. . .

Husband: Yeah, you're right.

Wife: All right, all right, let's forget about it for now.

Husband: I really am sorry.

CONVERSATION TOOLS

See the General Teaching Tips, page 6, for suggestions on teaching Conversation Tools.

6 ANSWERS

1. Husband: I'm sorry, I forgot to call you. / I know, I'm sorry. / It's my fault. / I apologize. / I really am sorry. / Let me make it up to you.

Wife: . . . let's forget about it for now. / OK, that sounds good.

C. REAL TALK: USE WHAT YOU'VE LEARNED (page 98)

Vocabulary Review

See the General Teaching Tips, page 6, for suggestions on conducting the vocabulary review.

2 ANSWERS

1. absent-mindedness	**3.** on my mind	**5.** scatterbrain
2. the end of the world	**4.** slipped my mind	**6.** make it up to you

Role Play

See the General Teaching Tips, page 7, for suggestions on conducting role plays.

Part Three: On the Air

Background

Students will hear an interview with Dr. Mel Levine, author of the book *All Kinds of Minds* and founder of the organization by the same name. For more information, visit http://www.allkindsofminds.org/index.aspx.

Art

See the General Teaching Tips, page 3, for suggestions on presenting art.

A. PRELISTENING (page 100)

See the General Teaching Tips, page 3, for suggestions on conducting prelistening speaking activities.

Partner Activity: Test Your Memory

1. Read the directions for the activity with the class and emphasize that students must follow them precisely. Do not model the activity.
2. You should be the timekeeper for the whole class. This will make it easier for students to count their partners' answers. Listeners can count on their fingers or use a sheet of paper and write lines or ticks for each word their partner recites. They should *not* write down their partners' words because that will take too much time.
3. After students discuss the activity with their partner, bring the whole class together and do a survey of students' answers. Write a selection of answers to question 2 in Exercise 2 on the board.

Vocabulary Preview

See the General Teaching Tips, page 4, for suggestions on conducting the vocabulary preview.

B. LISTENING (page 101)

Main Ideas

See the General Teaching Tips, page 4, for suggestions on teaching the Main Ideas section.

1 ANSWERS
1. c
2. recode (transform)
3. put information in categories

Details and Inferences

See the General Teaching Tips, page 4, for suggestions on teaching this section.

2 ANSWERS
1. a, b, d
2. put it into words, describe it
3. a. make a diagram of it; b. make a chart; c. picture it; d. think of examples of it

4. b, c, e

5. farm animals, wild animals (African or savanna), insects

6. c

7. a

Listening for Language

See the General Teaching Tips, page 5, for suggestions on teaching this section.

CONVERSATION TOOLS

See the General Teaching Tips, page 6, for suggestions on teaching Conversation Tools.

❹ ANSWERS

    1. filing system   **2.** files, folders

C. REAL TALK: USE WHAT YOU'VE LEARNED (page 104)

Vocabulary Review

See the General Teaching Tips, page 6, for suggestions on conducting the vocabulary review.

❷ ANSWERS

Synonyms: elaborate and extend; recode, modify, and transform

Discussion

1. See the General Teaching Tips, page 6, for suggestions on conducting discussions.
2. Other metaphors for memory might be a computer, a DVD, a bulletin board, a roadmap, a warehouse, a library, or any storage system that uses classification, such as a well-organized closet or desk.

Part Four: In Class

Art

1. The cartoon shows a man overwhelmed by a long list of new vocabulary he is supposed to learn.
2. See the General Teaching Tips, page 3, for suggestions on presenting art.

A. PRELISTENING (page 106)

See the General Teaching Tips, page 10, for suggestions on conducting prelistening activities in this part of the chapter.

Discussion

See the General Teaching Tips, page 6, for suggestions on conducting discussions.

Vocabulary Preview

See the General Teaching Tips, page 4, for suggestions on conducting the vocabulary preview.

B. LISTENING AND NOTE-TAKING (page 107)

See the General Teaching Tips, page 10, for suggestions on teaching this section.

Lecture Organization: Describing a Process or Technique

See the General Teaching Tips, page 11, for suggestions on teaching this section.

② ANSWERS
memory technique called mnemonics

Lecture Language: Hypothetical Situations

See the General Teaching Tips, page 11, for suggestions on teaching this section.

④ ANSWERS

1. Suppose, suppose
2. let's say
3. let's pretend
4. imagine

Taking Notes

See the General Teaching Tips, page 12, for suggestions on teaching this section.

⑥ SAMPLE OUTLINE

	I. Intro
	A. Previous lec.: Memory works by transforming info
topic	B. This lec.: Memory techniques = mnemonics
	C. Def: Systematic strats. to help us remember
examples	◯ e.g. numbers, lists, names, etc.
mnemonic technique	II. Keyword method
	A. History: Dev'd 30 yrs. ago by R. C. Atkinson
	B. Purpose: learn vocab in foreign lang.
	C. Ex: *kaposzta* (Hungarian)
	III. Steps
1st step	◯ A. Choose keyword
3 characteristics	1. Charac. of good keyword
	a. word you know well
	b. sounds like target word
	c. easy to visualize, e.g. concrete noun or verb
	2. Ex: kaposzta →cop

2nd step	B. Create mental image
	1. contains keyword + target meaning, i.e., cop + cabbage
	2. interacting
	3. best if moving, colorful, exaggerated, silly
example	4. Ex: cop w/cabbage head
3rd step	C. Focus on image to fix in memory
how to study	IV. How to study for test
	A. Ex: kaposzta → cop (key word) → cabbage
	B. "Cop" is bridge from kaposzta to cabbage
conclusion	V. Conclusion
	A. Research shows sts. who use keyword method remember vocab > sts. who don't
	B. Mnemon. not "magic." Still have to study.

Reviewing the Lecture

See the General Teaching Tips, page 13, for suggestions on conducting this activity.

C. REAL TALK: USE WHAT YOU'VE LEARNED (page 110)

See the General Teaching Tips, page 6, for suggestions on teaching this section.

Vocabulary Review

See the General Teaching Tips, pages 6, for suggestions on conducting the vocabulary review.

Practicing the Keyword Method

1. Make sure that students follow the steps in the keyword method to learn the new words. That is, they need to;
   * choose a keyword;
   * create a mental image that includes the keyword and the target word;
   * focus on the image to fix it in memory.
2. Have students share their keywords and images with their classmates. This will help fix the new words in their memories.
3. If possible, give the test on the words several days after the students complete Step 1. The test should be for fun; do not grade it.

TOEFL Practice

1. See the General Teaching Tips, page 14, for suggestions on conducting this activity.
2. Every student talk will be different, but a complete presentation should include the following:
   * the three characteristics of a good keyword;
   * the suggestion, stated in the reading passage, that keywords related to the target word in both sound and meaning are best;
   * one to two examples from the student's first language, including target words to be learned and suitable keywords for learning them.

Part One: In Person

Art

1. The photo shows a young woman who has a tattoo on her arm.
2. See the General Teaching Tips, page 3, for suggestions on presenting art.

A. PRELISTENING (page 113)

See the General Teaching Tips, page 3, for suggestions on conducting prelistening speaking activities.

Discussion

See the General Teaching Tips, page 6, for suggestions on conducting discussions.

Vocabulary Preview

See the General Teaching Tips, page 4, for suggestions on conducting the vocabulary preview.

B. LISTENING (page 114)

Main Ideas

See the General Teaching Tips, page 4, for suggestions on teaching the Main Ideas section.

❶ ANSWERS
1. a rose on her shoulder
2. They disapprove.
3. no

Details and Inferences

See the General Teaching Tips, page 4, for suggestions on teaching this section.

❷ ANSWERS
1. 16 or 17. She is allowed to drive in a car alone with a friend.

(continued)

2.

Jennifer's Arguments	Parents' Arguments
1. Tattoos are cool.	1. They don't care what other kids are doing.
2. Her parents allowed her to pierce her ears.	2. Pierced ears are different from tattoos.
3. She won't get tired of it.	3. Jennifer doesn't know how she's going to feel (about a tattoo) in 5–10 years.
4. She can have it removed.	4. Tattoo removal is painful and leaves scars.
5. Henna is for kids.	5. Jennifer can use henna instead.
6. She's a good girl and should be able to do what she wants.	6. Jennifer already gets to do most of what she wants.

3. a diamond stud in her nose

4. Mother: patient, tolerant, firm
Father: critical, sarcastic, firm, angry

Listening for Language

See the General Teaching Tips, page 5, for suggestions on teaching this section.

CONVERSATION TOOLS

See the General Teaching Tips, page 6, for suggestions on teaching Conversation Tools.

C. REAL TALK: USE WHAT YOU'VE LEARNED (page 116)

Vocabulary Review

See the General Teaching Tips, page 6, for suggestions on conducting the vocabulary review.

❷ ANSWERS

1. give me a hard time

2. for a change

3. thought this through

4. get tired of

5. fit in

6. on my own

7. for one thing . . . for another (thing)

Discussion

See the General Teaching Tips, page 6, for suggestions on conducting discussions.

Role Play

See the General Teaching Tips, page 7, for suggestions on conducting role plays.

Part Two: On the Phone

Art

1. The art shows a young man working in front of a computer and talking on the phone.
2. See the General Teaching Tips, page 3, for suggestions on presenting art.

A. PRELISTENING (page 118)

See the general Teaching Tips, page 3, for suggestions on conducting prelistening speaking activities.

Discussion

1. See the General Teaching Tips, page 6, for suggestions on conducting discussions.
2. Possible answer to the second bulleted question: Companies that produce make up, other beauty aids, and pharmaceuticals would benefit from the results of a survey about beauty. They would most likely ask questions relating to people's self-image and the products they use to look better.

Vocabulary Preview

See the General Teaching Tips, page 4, for suggestions on conducting the vocabulary preview.

B. LISTENING (page 119)

Main Ideas

See the General Teaching Tips, page 4, for suggestions on teaching the Main Ideas section.

❶ ANSWERS
1. Americans' attitudes about beauty and body image
2. a, b, d, e

Details and Inferences

See the General Teaching Tips, page 4, for suggestions on teaching this section.

❷ ANSWERS
2. 1. a   2. b   3. a   4. a   5. c   6. a
3. Age: 25–34
   Income: no answer
   Marital status: never married

Listening for Language

See the General Teaching Tips, page 5, for suggestions on teaching this section.

FOCUS ON SOUND

See the General Teaching Tips, page 5, for suggestions on teaching Focus on Sound.

CONVERSATION TOOLS

See the General Teaching Tips, page 6, for suggestions on teaching Conversation Tools.

⑦ SAMPLE ANSWERS

Answers will vary. For example:

In general, are you happy with your job?
Are you satisfied with your apartment, for the most part?
Does it generally rain a lot in the summer in [city]?
All in all did you like [name of movie]?
On the whole, what is your opinion of the president's decision to [verb]?
Where do you mainly shop for food?

C. REAL TALK: USE WHAT YOU'VE LEARNED (page 123)

Vocabulary Review

1. See the General Teaching Tips, page 6, for suggestions on conducting the vocabulary review.
2. Be sure to circulate as students are talking. Note cases where students both correctly and incorrectly use the vocabulary being reviewed.

Role Play

See the General Teaching Tips, page 7, for suggestions on conducting role plays.

Optional Extension Activity

Have students look at the archive of Gallup polls at http://www.galluppoll.com/. Have them choose a poll and report on it to the class.

Part Three: On the Air

Background

Plastic surgery is a multimillion-dollar industry in the United States. According to the American Society for Aesthetic Plastic Surgery (ASAPS), nearly 11.5 million cosmetic surgical and nonsurgical procedures were performed in the United States in 2005.

Art

1. The photo shows a woman's face being marked to indicate where the surgeon anticipates making incisions for her plastic surgery.
2. See the General Teaching Tips, page 3, for suggestions on presenting art.

A. PRELISTENING (page 124)

See the General Teaching Tips, page 3, for suggestions on conducting prelistening speaking activities.

Discussion

See the General Teaching Tips, page 6, for suggestions on conducting discussions.

Vocabulary Preview

See the General Teaching Tips, page 4, for suggestions on conducting the vocabulary preview.

B. LISTENING (page 125)

Main Ideas

See the General Teaching Tips, page 4, for suggestions on teaching the Main Ideas section.

❶ ANSWERS
1. She is in her late thirties.
2. She works in sales.
3. She had her eyes "refreshed" (to remove the bags under and over) and the bump taken out of her nose.
4. She wanted to look younger so that she could compete with young people in her industry.

Details and Inferences

See the General Teaching Tips, page 4, for suggestions on teaching this section.

❷ ANSWERS
1.

	Before Surgery	After Surgery
General appearance	washed out, tired, ready to go to bed	younger
Eyes	bags under and over	refreshed, awake
Nose	bump	more cosmetically pleasing
Self-esteem	felt bad about herself, didn't want to go for interviews	fired up, ready to go, can do anything, conquer anything

(continued)

2. a. False. She says her company is not in great shape; "the handwriting is on the wall."

b. False. She says she is *about* to be unemployed.

c. False. She had no trouble at all.

d. False. She had surgery to remove a bump in her nose.

e. True. She says she has seen young people "bump out" people in their forties and fifties.

3. a

Listening for Language

See the General Teaching Tips, page 5, for suggestions on teaching this section.

CONVERSATION TOOLS

See the General Teaching Tips, page 6, for suggestions on teaching Conversation Tools.

④ ANSWERS

1. Absolutely, Yeah	**3.** Yeah
2. Yes, absolutely	**4.** Yes

⑤ SAMPLE ANSWERS

Answers will vary. For example:

Do you think it's OK for men to have plastic surgery?

Is plastic surgery safe?

Does age discrimination exist in your native country or culture?

Should national health insurance pay for people to have plastic surgery?

C. REAL TALK: USE WHAT YOU'VE LEARNED (page 128)

Vocabulary Review

1. See the General Teaching Tips, page 6, for suggestions on conducting the vocabulary review.

2. Be sure to circulate as students are talking. Note cases where students both correctly and incorrectly use the vocabulary being reviewed.

② ANSWERS

1. Mr. Assad's company is <u>not in great shape</u>.

2. <u>The handwriting is on the wall</u>.

3. Jackie looked <u>washed out</u> . . .

4. . . . to correct the <u>bump</u> in his nose.

5. . . . Mrs. Linden felt <u>fired up</u>.

6. . . . full of <u>dot-commers</u> . . .

7. . . . their plastic surgery <u>boosted their self-esteem</u>.

Discussion

1. See the General Teaching Tips, page 6, for suggestions on conducting discussions.

2. Point out to students the trends in the chart about cosmetic surgery procedures:

- A country's rank is not correlated with its wealth. For example, Mexico is ranked No. 2 for percentage of procedures worldwide, but it is not a wealthy country. Belgium, with a very high per capita income, is ranked No. 15.
- The top five ranked countries are all in the Americas.

3. *Optional:* Have students predict which country would be No. 16. Also ask if any information in the chart surprises them (perhaps that China does not appear in the top 15). Have students do Internet research to try to find more recent rankings. One source of information is the International Society of Aesthetic Plastic Surgery, http://www.isaps.org/.

Part Four: In Class

Background

Most discussions about beauty are about women. The lecture in this section, by contrast, is about "body image perceptions in men"—that is, how men see or perceive their own bodies.

Art

1. The art shows contrasting images of men from two cultures, the United States and China. The American man is more muscular than the Chinese.
2. See the General Teaching Tips, page 3, for suggestions on presenting art.

A. PRELISTENING (page 130)

See the General Teaching Tips, page 10, for suggestions on conducting prelistening activities in this part of the chapter.

Discussion

1. See the General Teaching Tips, page 6, for suggestions on conducting discussions.
2. *Bulimia* is a medical condition in which a person eats extremely large amounts of food in a short time and then vomits intentionally. *Anorexia* is an illness in which a person refuses to eat over a long period of time, resulting in dangerous, sometimes fatal, weight loss. Both bulimia and anorexia are examples of *body image disorders* in which the person suffering from the condition believes, unrealistically, that he or she is too fat.
3. Other body image disorders involve a person's obsession with a particular body part, such as one's nose or stomach, and the belief that this part is abnormal or unattractive in the extreme.

Vocabulary Preview

See the General Teaching Tips, page 4, for suggestions on conducting the vocabulary preview.

B. LISTENING AND NOTE-TAKING (page 131)

See the General Teaching Tips, page 10, for suggestions on teaching this section.

Lecture Organization and Language: Research Reports

1. See the General Teaching Tips, page 11, for suggestions on teaching this section.
2. It will be easier for students to understand the information in the chart if you provide a context. Choose a research study with which you are familiar. (For instance, you could copy a research article from a professional journal such as the *TESOL Quarterly*.) Discuss what information was or would be included in the Introduction, Method, Results, and Discussion sections.
3. Invite students to describe research studies from their own fields.

❷ ANSWERS

Sentence	Part	Cues
1	Introduction	Present perfect tense Review of what the course has already covered
2	Introduction	Questions the researchers wanted to investigate
3	Introduction	Subjects of the study
4	Method	What the researchers did (past tense)
5	Method	"the next phase of the study"
6	Results	What the researchers found
7	Discussion	The researchers "interpreted"
8	Discussion	"Another explanation could be . . ." (modal of possibility)

Lecture Language: Expressions of Contrast

See the General Teaching Tips, page 11, for suggestions on teaching this section.

❹ SAMPLE ANSWERS

Answers will vary. For example:

1. What the researchers found were two <u>significant differences . . .</u>

2. . . . underdeveloped, <u>whereas</u> the Taiwanese men . . .
3. . . . average. <u>Yet</u> . . .
4. <u>In contrast</u> / <u>Conversely</u>, the Taiwanese men . . .
5. . . . generation. This <u>contrasts with</u> Chinese culture, . . .

Taking Notes

1. See the General Teaching Tips, page 12, for suggestions on teaching this section.
2. In Exercise 5, follow the directions in the book precisely. Students should take notes on their own paper. They should then edit and rewrite their notes in the book.
3. *Optional:* Instead of having students take notes in outline form, they can do so in a chart, like the following:

Introduction	Methods	Results	Discussion

Another option is a two-column format, like the following:

Introduction	
Methods	
Results	
Discussion	

⑤ SAMPLE OUTLINE

		I. Intro
		A. Previous topic: Body image disorders in women
topic	◯	B. This lec. topic: Body image disord. in men
		1. 1-2% of Western men have it
		2. Expressed as:
		a. obsession w/ bodybuilding
		b. use of steroids
		3. Contrast: East Asian cultures: (a) + (b) rare
new study		II. New study
where		A. At McLean Hosp., Boston
research question		B. Question: Why cult. diff. exists
subjects		C. Subjects = College men in U.S., France, Austria

(continued)

method	**III. Method**
	A. showed pics. of men w/ diff. levels of muscle
	B. Asked subs to choose 4 images =
	1. their body
	2. average body (their culture)
	3. ideal body
	4. body women prefer
	C. Also asked women to choose ideal body
	D. Repeated proced. w/ subs from Taiwan
	E. Analyzed data for sim. and diff.
results	**IV. Results: 2 sig. diffs.**
	A. Ideal body image
	1. West. men said ideal body = 13 kg > their weight
	2. Taiwan. men: only 2 kg >
interpretation	West. men dissatisfied w/ body, Taiw. men satisfied
	B. Body women preferred
	1. West. men said: 30 lb (14 kg) more musc. than theirs
	BUT women picked aver. body, no musc.
	2. Taiw. men said: aver. body, like theirs
	Taiw. women picked same
conclusion	C. Findings suggest: West. men have distorted view of ideal body,
	Taiwanese men don't
discussion	**V. Why? 3 hypotheses**
1st hypothesis	A. Def. of masc.
	1. West. cult. use muscles to measure masc.
	2. Chinese use intellect, character
2nd hypothesis	B. Media influence
	1. More images of undressed, musc. men in West than
	2. Taiwan → less exposore to "ideal body"
3rd hypothesis	C. Trad. male roles changing
	1. West: More women work → men use muscles for self-esteem
	2. Taiwan: More men still in trad. role of breadwinner →
	more secure

Reviewing the Lecture

See the General Teaching Tips, page 13, for suggestions on conducting this activity.

C. REAL TALK: USE WHAT YOU'VE LEARNED (page 136)

See the General Teaching Tips, page 6, for suggestions on teaching this section.

Vocabulary Review

See the General Teaching Tips, pages 6, for suggestions on conducting the vocabulary review.

❷ ANSWERS
1. Steroid abuse
2. distorted, bodybuilding, bulked up
3. With respect to
4. account for
5. In short

Discussion

See the General Teaching tips, page 6, for suggestions on conducting discussions.

Research Report

1. See the General Teaching tips, page 8, for suggestions on conducting oral reports or presentations; see page 9 for a sample peer evaluation form.
2. *Note:* Commercial Internet sites generally end with *.com,* whereas educational or nonprofit sites end with *.edu or .org.* U.S. government sites, such as the National Institutes of Health, end with *.gov.* Caution students that they may find useful information at *.com* sites, but they should be aware of the advertising on these sites and verify any material they find.

TOEFL Practice

1. See the General Teaching Tips, page 14, for suggestions on conducting this activity.
2. Every student talk will be different, but a complete presentation will include the following:
   - The basic finding of the McLean Hospital study was that Western men were generally dissatisfied with their bodies, but Taiwanese men were satisfied.
   - American men mistakenly predicted women would prefer a body more muscular than theirs, but Taiwanese men predicted correctly that women would choose an "average" body like theirs.
   - Studies in several Asian countries of female body image showed that women were satisfied with their bodies until they were exposed to Western media.
   - Thus it is logical to conclude that if the McLean Hospital study on men is repeated in ten years, the Asian men will also show dissatisfaction with their bodies following years of exposure to Western media.

CHAPTER 6

DISCOVERIES

Part One: In Person

Background

The topic of space exploration is one that students may not have had much exposure to prior to this lesson. Use the background information and the art to generate interest and excitement in the topic. For additional information and multimedia presentations, direct students to the NASA home page at http://www.nasa.gov/home/. For additional information about the mission to Mars and spectacular photos, type "Mars rover" in the search box.

Art

1. It is hard to tell from the photo, but the Mars rovers are small—less than 5 feet tall and 3 to 4 feet wide.
2. See the General Teaching Tips, page 3, for suggestions on presenting art.

A. PRELISTENING (page 139)

See the General Teaching Tips, page 3, for suggestions on conducting prelistening speaking activities.

Discussion

See the General Teaching Tips, page 6, for suggestions on conducting discussions.

Vocabulary Preview

See the General Teaching Tips, page 4, for suggestions on conducting the vocabulary preview.

B. LISTENING (page 140)
Main Ideas

See the General Teaching Tips, page 4, for suggestions on teaching the Main Ideas section.

❶ ANSWERS
1. water or signs of past water
2. geological evidence of water millions of years ago
3. It could indicate whether Mars is habitable, i.e., whether people could live there someday.
4. going back to places where there might have been water and doing a sophisticated chemical analysis of the soil to find out what minerals there were and whether they were conducive to life

Details and Inferences

See the General Teaching Tips, page 4, for suggestions on teaching this section.

❷ ANSWERS

1. a   **2.** c   **3.** a   **4.** b   **5.** c   **6.** d

Listening for Language

See the General Teaching Tips, page 5, for suggestions on teaching this section.

FOCUS ON SOUND

1. See the General Teaching Tips, page 5, for suggestions on teaching Focus on Sound.
2. Sentences containing past modals and unreal conditionals are long, and even advanced students may have trouble producing them. Allow time in this lesson for repetition and drill.

❹ ANSWERS

1. may have been
2. might be
3. could have been, might find, could be, could live
4. might have been, would they have been
5. would have discovered

CONVERSATION TOOLS

1. See the General Teaching Tips, page 6, for suggestions on teaching Conversaton Tools.
2. You can find many more urban myths at www.snopes.com.

C. REAL TALK: USE WHAT YOU'VE LEARNED (page 144)

Vocabulary Review

1. See the General Teaching Tips, page 6, for suggestions on conducting the vocabulary review.
2. Be sure to circulate as students are talking. Note cases where students both correctly and incorrectly use the vocabulary being reviewed.

❷ ANSWERS

1. mission	**4.** mineral	**7.** site
2. distinctive	**5.** gut feeling	**8.** conducive
3. habitable	**6.** microbes	**9.** drop in the bucket

Discussion: The Pros and Cons of Space Exploration

See the General Teaching Tips, page 6, for suggestions on conducting discussions.

Answers will vary. Here are some arguments for and against space exploration:

Pro

1. The desire to explore is an innate human characteristic that has led us to many important discoveries on Earth.
2. We should explore the option of living in space in case Earth becomes uninhabitable as a result of nuclear war, pollution, or overpopulation.
3. Other planets may have resources that are needed on Earth.

Con

1. Satellites and space vehicles orbiting around the Earth create "space pollution."
2. Space exploration is too expensive.
3. Space travel is dangerous.
4. Vehicles traveling back to Earth from distant planets could inadvertently bring back dangerous microbes that harm people.

Part Two: On the Phone

Art

1. The family tree may require further explanation, or you may need to get students interested in the topic. You might want to sketch your own family tree on the board and spend a few minutes telling the class about your family.
2. See the General Teaching Tips, page 3, for suggestions on presenting art.

A. PRELISTENING (page 147)

See the General Teaching Tips, page 3, for suggestions on conducting prelistening speaking activities.

Discussion

See the General Teaching Tips, page 6, for suggestions on conducting discussions.

Vocabulary Preview

See the General Teaching Tips, page 4, for suggestions on conducting the vocabulary preview.

B. LISTENING (page 147)

Background

You can explain the difference between first cousins and first cousins once removed as follows: John and Mary are brother and sister. John has a son named Jack. Mary has a daughter named Mona. Jack and Mona are first cousins. If Jack has a daughter named Jill, then Jill and Mona are first cousins once removed. Finally, if Mona has a son named Andrew, then Jill and Andrew are second cousins.

The best way to make these relationships clear is to draw a family tree on the board as you explain the terms.

Main Ideas

1. See the General Teaching Tips, page 4, for suggestions on teaching the Main Ideas section.
2. The man's last name, Knoop, is pronounced like "knope (k-nōp)."

❶ ANSWERS

1. Boston. He's in town on business.
2. no
3. They are first cousins once removed. Brent and Rose's mother are first cousins.
4. He found a picture of her on the Internet.

Details and Inferences

See the General Teaching Tips, page 4, for suggestions on teaching this section.

❷ ANSWERS

1.

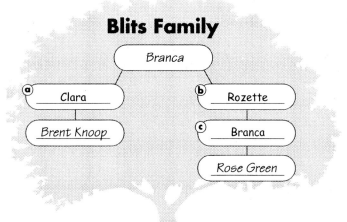

2. a. Rose's grandmother (Rozette) and Brent's mother (Clara)
   b. Branca and Brent
   c. Rose and Brent
   d. Branca
3. confused
4. mentally alert

FOCUS ON SOUND

1. See the General Teaching Tips, page 5, for suggestions on teaching Focus on Sound.
2. *Note*: English has many more consonant clusters than most other languages. Your students may speak languages that have fewer or different consonant clusters than English has. As a result, they may drop one or more consonants from a cluster (e.g., "steet" instead of "street") or insert vowels before or between the consonants in the cluster (e.g., Spanish and Farsi speakers insert an "e" at the beginning of English words that begin with "st" or "str").

④ ANSWERS

1. nd in "sound"	**4.** nd in "find"	**7.** n't in "don't"
2. rst in "first"	**5.** xt in "next"	**8.** ft in "left"
3. ndm in "grandmother"	**6.** nd in "found"	

⑤ ANSWERS

1. You can always find me at this number.

2. My first cousins live in lots of different cities.

3. I don't feel comfortable using her first name.

4. I'm going to bring my grandmother some chocolate.

5. Joseph left for work several minutes ago.

6. On your next visit, tell me more about your family.

7. What's wrong with that piano? It sounds strange.

C. REAL TALK: USE WHAT YOU'VE LEARNED (page 150)

Vocabulary Review

1. See the General Teaching Tips, page 6, for suggestions on conducting the vocabulary review.
2. Be sure to circulate as students are talking. Note cases where students both correctly and incorrectly use the vocabulary being reviewed.

② ANSWERS

1. as sharp as a tack	**4.** head was spinning	**7.** obsession
2. Google	**5.** high school reunion	**8.** detective
3. coincidence	**6.** genealogy	

Discussion

See the General Teaching Tips, page 6, for suggestions on conducting discussions.

Role Play

See the General Teaching Tips, page 7, for suggestions on conducting role plays.

Part Three: On the Air

Background

The *Motley Fool* is a radio program that deals with money matters. For more information, visit http://www.fool.com/.

Art

1. *Note*: People buy metal detectors mainly for the purpose of searching for coins at the beach, a park, etc. The machines emit noise when they detect metal objects. These two photos show a man's ring, which is the type of object a metal detector can locate, and a person using a detector on a beach.
2. See the General Teaching Tips, page 3, for suggestions on presenting art.

A. PRELISTENING (page 153)

See the General Teaching Tips, page 3, for suggestions on conducting prelistening speaking activities.

Discussion

See the General Teaching Tips, page 6, for suggestions on conducting discussions.

Vocabulary Preview

See the General Teaching Tips, page 4, for suggestions on conducting the vocabulary preview.

B. LISTENING (page 153)
Main Ideas

See the General Teaching Tips, page 4, for suggestions on teaching the Main Ideas section.

① ANSWERS
1. a man's diamond and sapphire ring   3. He still has it.
2. with a metal detector

Details and Inferences

See the General Teaching Tips, page 4, for suggestions on teaching this section.

② ANSWERS
1. a, c   2. c, d   3. 1. b; 2. a; 3. d; 4. c

Listening for Language

See the General Teaching Tips, page 5, for suggestions on teaching this section.

FOCUS ON SOUND

See the General Teaching Tips, page 5, for suggestions on teaching Focus on Sound.

④ ANSWERS
1. getting, going to   2. kind of   3. Because   4. people would be coming

CONVERSATION TOOLS

See the General Teaching Tips, page 6, for suggestions on teaching Conversation Tools.

⑥ ANSWERS
1. the hosts   3. at any rate
2. Doug's cell phone   4. Back to the metal detector

C. REAL TALK: USE WHAT YOU'VE LEARNED (page 156)

Vocabulary Review

1. See the General Teaching Tips, page 6, for suggestions on conducting the vocabulary review.
2. Be sure to circulate as students are talking. Note cases where students both correctly and incorrectly use the vocabulary being reviewed.

Discussion

1. See the General Teaching Tips, page 6, for suggestions on conducting discussions.
2. *Optional*: Do a follow-up discussion about the conditions under which students would feel obligated to try to return a found object to its owner.

Role Play

See the General Teaching Tips, page 7, for suggestions on conducting role plays.

Part Four: In Class

Background

The lecture in this chapter challenges the traditional image of Christopher Columbus as the man who discovered America. It also presents an unconventional point of view regarding the impact of the European colonization on the native peoples residing in the Americas at the end of the fifteenth and beginning of the sixteenth centuries.

Art

1. This portrait of Christopher Columbus was painted by the Italian Sebastiano del Piombo sometime after the year 1500.
2. See the General Teaching Tips, page 3, for suggestions on presenting art.

A. PRELISTENING (page 159)

See the General Teaching Tips, page 10, for suggestions on conducting prelistening activities in this part of the chapter.

QUIZ ANSWERS

1. F (He was Italian.)
2. T
3. T
4. F (Isabella and her husband, King Ferdinand, were Spanish.)
5. T
6. F (The first was a Scandinavian, Leif Ericsson.)
7. F (He sent slaves from America to Europe.)
8. T

Vocabulary Preview

See the General Teaching Tips, page 4, for suggestions on conducting the vocabulary preview.

B. LISTENING AND NOTE-TAKING (page 160)

See the General Teaching Tips, page 10, for suggestions on teaching this section.

Lecture Organization: Making Assertions and Providing Proof

See the General Teaching Tips, page 11, for suggestions on teaching this section.

❷ SAMPLE ANSWERS

Answers will vary. For example:

1. Columbus did not discover America.
2. Columbus never set foot in North America.
3. Columbus did not prove that the Earth was round.

Lecture Language: Signaling Proof

1. See the General Teaching Tips, page 11, for suggestions on teaching this section.

❹ ANSWERS

1. How do we know this?

   . . . and the archaeological evidence is clear that . . .
2. on the basis of those (written records)
3. written records show that . . .

❺ SAMPLE ANSWER

Answers will vary. For example:

"In 1492, educated people already knew that the Earth was round. How do we know this? Well, first, the monastery of St. Catherine in the Sinai peninsula has a religious statue painted 500 years before Columbus, showing Jesus ruling over a spherical earth. Second, records show that already in the tenth century, Arab scientists had described the Earth as a sphere with 360 degrees of longitude and 180 degrees of latitude."

Taking Notes

1. See the General Teaching Tips, page 12, for suggestions on teaching this section.
2. In Exercise 6, follow the directions in the book precisely. Students should take notes on their own paper. Afterward, they should edit and rewrite their notes in the book.

⑥ SAMPLE OUTLINE

topic		I. Topic: Discoveries of Christopher Columbus
4 facts	○	Italian explorer and trader
		born 1451
		1492: sailed west to try to reach Asia
		landed in Carib, believed = India
		II. Americans give C. credit for:
2 discoveries		disc. America
		proving earth is round
		III. Both beliefs = false
1st assertion		A. C. did not disc. America
proof		1. Proof
	○	• 20,000 yrs ago Asia + No. Amer. connected by land
		• 1st inhab. arrived in N. Amer. from Asia at that time
		• DNA evidence → these people = ancestors of all
		Amer. tribes
		2. C. not even 1st European to reach Amer.
		• 1st = Scandinavian explorer, Leif Ericsson,
		landed in no. east Canada 1000AD
		3. C. kept records, showed he never set foot in No. Amer.
		• 4 voyages: 1492, 1493, 1498, and 1502
		• Closest to Amer. = Bahamas
2nd assertion		B. C. did not prove Earth = round
proof		1. Greeks knew 2,000 yrs. ago
	○	2. 1492 Euros knew
		3. No doubt C. knew

3 positive accomplishments	**IV. What did C. accomplish?**
	A. Estab. cult. & econ. link between Euro & Amer.
○	B. Initiate trade
	C. Bring Christianity to Amer.
result	D. These accomps → Amer. consider C. great hero
3 negative accomplishments	**V. C.'s arrival disastrous for Native Amer.**
	A. Started slavery as way to repay Spanish king/queen
	for financing voyage
	B. Captured natives & forced them to work in mines
	& plantations; killed those who resisted
○	After 4 yrs., 1/3 of native pop. killed or exported
	C. Brought disease, esp. smallpox → killed 1,000s
conclusion	**VI. Many people today say this is C.'s true legacy**

Reviewing the Lecture

See the General Teaching Tips, page 13, for suggestions on conducting this activity.

C. REAL TALK: USE WHAT YOU'VE LEARNED (page 164)

See the General Teaching Tips, page 6, for suggestions on teaching this section.

Vocabulary Review

See the General Teaching Tips, pages 6, for suggestions on conducting the vocabulary review.

Survey

See the General Teaching Tips, pages 8, for suggestions on conducting interviews and surveys. See the instructions there for options in the event that there are no English speakers for your students to interview.

TOEFL Practice

1. See the General Teaching Tips, page 14, for suggestions on conducting this activity.

2. Every student talk will be different. Make sure students answer the question and support their opinion with reasons and facts. For example, a student might say that Columbus's 1492 arrival in the Caribbean was the event that had the greatest impact on history because it opened the door to European colonization of the Americas, which in turn brought Christianity to the New World and forged relations between the Americas and the rest of the world. Another student might argue that, for better or for worse, the arrival of Christianity in the Americas was the event that had the greatest impact on history since today, Christianity is the most widely practiced religion in the world.

CHAPTER 7 LAW AND ORDER

Part One: In Person

Background

In this part of the chapter, students will hear a woman talking about her experience as a member of a jury in a criminal trial. For information about the U.S. jury system, check an online information source such as Wikipedia.

Art

1. The photo shows a typical courtroom scene. The members of the jury sit in the jury box, which is on the left. The woman speaking to them is an attorney. The man behind her is an officer of the court (similar to a police officer). On the right, the man in the box with the American flag is the judge. In front of him, in the center of the photo, the woman typing is the court stenographer. The two tables in the foreground of the photo are for the defense and prosecution teams, respectively. The person accused of a crime sits with the defense attorney.
2. See the General Teaching Tips, page 3, for suggestions on presenting art.

A. PRELISTENING (page 167)

1. See the General Teaching Tips, page 3, for suggestions on conducting prelistening speaking activities.
2. Have students read the information in the Background section silently. List the following terms on the board and have students describe or define each one: *jury, accused, judge, attorneys, witnesses, defense, prosecution, jury duty, trial, juror.*

Discussion

1. See the General Teaching Tips, page 6, for suggestions on conducting discussions.
2. One of the activities in the Real Talk section is Viewing Courtroom Scenes in Movies, page 173. If your students have no background knowledge at all about what happens in a U.S. court, you may wish to do this activity before listening.

Vocabulary Preview

1. See the General Teaching Tips, page 4, for suggestions on conducting the vocabulary preview.
2. The vocabulary preview for this chapter is longer than usual because it includes many words and expressions related to the law. As an optional activity, you might want to do a group brainstorm with the class to find out what students already know. Use a graphic organizer like the ones shown on page 54 of the Student Book to record students' ideas.

B. LISTENING (page 168)

Main Ideas

See the General Teaching Tips, page 4, for suggestions on teaching the Main Ideas section.

❶ ANSWERS

The defendant: a poorly educated, down-and-out young man
The victims / witnesses: some security guards or bicycle officers
The charge: assault (attacking the officers with a bottle)
The verdict: guilty

Details and Inferences

See the General Teaching Tips, page 4, for suggestions on teaching this section.

❷ ANSWERS

1. The speaker felt sympathy for the defendant. She says all the jurors felt sorry for him and her "heart went out to him." She also uses the phrase "bless his heart" and says he was "pathetic."
2. pathetic, unhealthy, beat up, inarticulate, poorly educated
3. The judge fell asleep.
4. a. True.
   b. False. The attorney who represents the accused person is called a defense attorney.
   c. True.
   d. False. They must follow the law.
   e. False. The jury is alone during deliberations.
   f. False. Juries are made up of diverse types of people.
   g. True.
5. a. unfortunate, poor, defeated
   b. very shabby, cheap, dirty
   c. boring, wordy; talking endlessly
   d. a case in which it is easy for the jury to determine guilt or innocence

Listening for Language

See the General Teaching Tips, page 5, for suggestions on teaching this section.

FOCUS ON SOUND

1. See the General Teaching Tips, page 5, for suggestions on teaching Focus on Sound.
2. The variety of English (SAE) described in this section is used by some country singers and by a great many characters in movies. In reality, though, it is spoken by a relatively small number of Americans. Therefore, while it is helpful for students to be able to understand SAE, there is no need for them to practice speaking with this dialect.

❹ ANSWERS

1. The case was about this down-and-out young man.
2. he was arrested and charged with assault.

3. . . . one of the bottles hit one of the officers in the arm.

4. . . . the officer came to trial with his arm in a sling.

5. He was pretty pathetic, poor fellow.

6. We all kind of felt sorry for him.

7. And in a way my heart went out to him.

CONVERSATION TOOLS

See the General Teaching Tips, page 6, for suggestions on teaching this section.

⑥ SAMPLE ANSWERS

Answers will vary. For example:

1. The robber was pretty pathetic, poor guy.

2. My heart goes out to his girlfriend.

3. I feel sorry for the victims. They must have been really scared.

4. I feel bad for the officers who tried to arrest him.

C. REAL TALK: USE WHAT YOU'VE LEARNED (page 172)

Vocabulary Review

1. See the General Teaching Tips, page 6, for suggestions on conducting the vocabulary review.
2. Be sure to circulate as students are talking. Note cases where students both correctly and incorrectly use the vocabulary being reviewed.
3. *Optional:* Conduct a simple game to help students review the vocabulary. Write each vocabulary item on a separate index card. Distribute one card to each student. Instruct students to write the definition of the item on the back of the card. Have students stand up and circulate to quiz one another on the terms on their cards. Tell them they need to try to talk to everyone in the class in the time allotted.

Interview / Research

1. See the General Teaching Tips, page 8, for suggestions on conducting interviews.
2. If an interview is not possible, have students look for court cases in news magazines and newspapers, which are written for the public and thus do not include many technical details. The website http://www.infoplease.com has summaries of important U.S. Supreme Court cases.

Part Two: On the Phone

Art

1. Ask students to describe what they see. Then ask them to say what probably happened just before the scene in the photo occurred. Finally, ask them what they think is going to happen next.
2. See the General Teaching Tips, page 3, for suggestions on presenting art.

A. PRELISTENING (page 174)

See the General Teaching Tips, page 3, for suggestions on conducting prelistening speaking activities.

Discussion

See the General Teaching Tips, page 6, for suggestions on conducting discussions.

Vocabulary Preview

See the General Teaching Tips, page 4, for suggestions on conducting the vocabulary preview.

B. LISTENING (page 174)

Main Ideas

See the General Teaching Tips, page 4, for suggestions on teaching the Main Ideas section.

❶ ANSWERS

1. a hit-and-run accident

2. a person driving a white van

3. a lady

4. the suspect drove away

Details and Inferences

See the General Teaching Tips, page 4, for suggestions on teaching this section.

❷ ANSWERS

1.

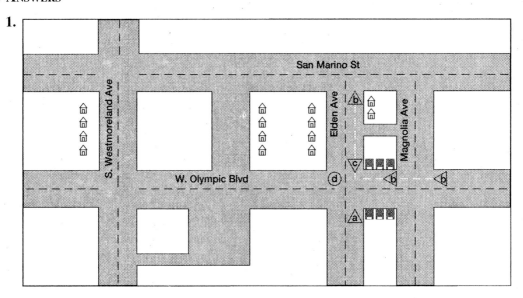

2. a. T

　　b. U

　　c. T

　　d. U

　　e. T

　　f. F

　　g. U

Listening for Language

See the General Teaching Tips, page 5, for suggestions on teaching this section.

FOCUS ON SOUND

See the General Teaching Tips, page 5, for suggestions on teaching Focus on Sound.

④ ANSWERS

1. the intersection
2. yesterday afternoon
3. I understand
4. show up
5. now and then
6. snow and ice
7. three elephants

CONVERSATION TOOLS

See the General Teaching Tips, page 6, for suggestions on teaching this section.

⑤ SAMPLE ANSWERS

Answers will vary. For example:

Topics for Student A

1. To begin with, I thought English was difficult, but on second thought I think it's not really that hard.
2. At first, I thought Sally was a snob, but after thinking it over, I realize she's just shy.
3. Originally, I wanted to buy an SUV, but after going back and forth about it, I decided to get something smaller.

Topics for Student B

1. Initially, I was going to vote for President (name), but after going over it in my mind, I've decide to vote for the other candidate.
2. Originally, I thought it would be cool to live in Hawaii, but on second thought, after visiting, I decided I didn't want to live on an island.
3. At first, I thought it was quite strange that Japanese people always remove their shoes when they enter someone's home, but after going over it in my mind, I came to appreciate this custom and continued practicing it even after I came back to the United States.

C. REAL TALK: USE WHAT YOU'VE LEARNED (page 178)

Vocabulary Review

1. See the General Teaching Tips, page 6, for suggestions on conducting the vocabulary review.
2. Be sure to circulate as students are talking. Note cases where students both correctly and incorrectly use the vocabulary being reviewed.

Role Play

1. See the General Teaching Tips, page 7, for suggestions on conducting role plays.
2. Explain to students that the pictures show only the *aftermath* of each accident, that is, the car smashed against a tree and the bicycle rider lying on the ground. Students playing the role of witnesses will need to make up the details of what caused the accidents. Encourage them to imagine where they were, what they were doing, and what they saw just prior to the accidents. Students playing the role of the detective should ask questions about these same details.

⊕ SAMPLE ANSWERS

Answers will vary. For example:

Scenario 1: The witness had been out walking his dog and saw the smashed car driving toward him. It was going somewhat faster than the speed limit. Suddenly a cat ran into the street. The driver swerved to avoid hitting the cat and drove the car into a tree.

Scenario 2: The witness was out walking. She saw the bicycle rider entering the intersection legally on a green light. A car made a right turn against the red light and hit the bicycle rider. The driver then drove away. The witness did not see the license number of the car.

You Be the Judge

1. The following questions may guide students in deciding on the driver's punishment:
   * Should the driver go to jail? If so, for how long?
   * Should he be required to pay any money to the family of the woman he struck?
   * Should he be required to attend an alcohol rehabilitation program?
2. Give students a time limit for their discussion, and tell them that they must reach a unanimous decision.

Part Three: On the Air

Background

The terms *panhandler, beggar,* and *homeless person* have slightly different uses in American English. A panhandler is someone who overtly asks a passersby for money. A beggar does the same thing, but this word is seldom used anymore. As for homeless people, they need money, but many of them are not panhandlers.

Art

1. The photo shows an unfortunately common sight in North America: a person begging for money from people passing by on the street.
2. See the General Teaching Tips, page 3, for suggestions on presenting art.

A. PRELISTENING (page 180)

See the General Teaching Tips, page 3, for suggestions on conducting prelistening speaking activities.

Discussion

See the General Teaching Tips, page 6, for suggestions on conducting discussions.

Vocabulary Preview

See the General Teaching Tips, page 4, for suggestions on conducting the vocabulary preview.

B. LISTENING (page 181)
Main Ideas

See the General Teaching Tips, page 4, for suggestions on teaching the Main Ideas section.

❶ ANSWERS

1. Some people panhandle because they really need the money.
2. It would make panhandling illegal in downtown Atlanta.

Details and Inferences

See the General Teaching Tips, page 4, for suggestions on teaching this section.

❷ ANSWERS

1.

Speaker	For or Against the Ordinance?	Reason
Murphy Davis, Open Door	against	"the criminalization of poverty"
Tony Singfield, Martin Luther King Campaign for Economic Justice	against	violation of poor people's freedom of speech and right to exist
Lamar Willis, City Council member	for	panhandling keeps people away from downtown and threatens business
A. J. Robinson, Central Atlantic Progress	for	people complain that panhandling makes them feel unsafe

(continued)

2. a. F
   b. T
   c. F
   d. T
   e. T
3. b

Listening for Language

See the General Teaching Tips, page 5, for suggestions on teaching this section.

FOCUS ON SOUND

See the General Teaching Tips, page 5, for suggestions on teaching Focus on Sound.

④ ANSWERS

2. questionnáire	**10.** Lebańese
3. ridículous	**11.** critíque
4. photógraphy	**12.** homógeneous
5. educátional	**13.** reálity
6. unháppiness	**14.** legislátion
7. indecísion	**15.** illégal
8. neíghborhood	**16.** ménacing
9. déstiny	

⑤ SAMPLE ANSWERS

Answers will vary. For example:

1. powerful, exciting, friendly
2. Chinese, grotesque, career
3. imagination, heroic, universal

C. REAL TALK: USE WHAT YOU'VE LEARNED (page 184)

Vocabulary Review

1. See the General Teaching Tips, page 6, for suggestions on conducting the vocabulary review.
2. The items in Exercise 2 contain the vocabulary from the review box. Students should use the vocabulary as they discuss the items.
3. *Optional activity for Exercise 2:* Cut the sentences into strips and distribute them to students. Have students give one-minute speeches in which they explain why they either agree or disagree with the statements.

Role Play: A City Council Meeting

1. See the General Teaching Tips, page 7, for suggestions on conducting role plays.
2. The members of the city council have the following tasks and responsibilities:

- <u>Mayor</u>: the head of the town; the person who opens and closes the meeting.
- <u>Secretary</u>: the person who writes down what occurs at the meeting. If there's a question about who said what, the secretary provides this information. In this role play, prior to the city council vote (Step 2e), the secretary should summarize the arguments that have been presented on both sides of the issue.
- <u>Treasurer</u>: the person in charge of the city's finances. Most city council meetings have a treasurer's report. In this role play, the treasurer should ask speakers questions concerning the cost of whatever they propose.
- <u>Parliamentarian</u>: the person who keeps track of whose turn it is to speak. In an actual city council meeting there are strict rules about this. In this activity, it can be the parliamentarian's job to make sure everyone gets a turn to speak and that speakers do not interrupt one another.

Part Four: In Class

Background

The speaker in this section is a professor at a college in Canada. That is why he supports his main ideas with information about Canada.

Note: The original lecture included three causes of crime, but here we have included only the first two.

Art

1. The photo shows the watchtower and fence surrounding a prison.
2. See the General Teaching Tips, page 3, for suggestions on presenting art.

A. PRELISTENING (page 186)

1. See the General Teaching Tips, page 10, for suggestions on conducting prelistening activities in this part of the chapter.
2. The term "white-collar crime" refers to nonviolent crimes committed by persons such as high-level company executives and politicians. Such crimes almost always involve large sums of money.

Vocabulary Preview

See the General Teaching Tips, page 4, for suggestions on conducting the vocabulary preview.

B. LISTENING AND NOTE-TAKING (page 186)

See the General Teaching Tips, page 10, for suggestions on teaching this section.

Lecture Organization: Cause and Effect

See the General Teaching Tips, page 11, for suggestions on teaching this section.

② ANSWERS

   1. a

   2. Topic: Causes of crime

      3 theories:

         I.

         II.

         III.

     (or A., B., C.)

Lecture Language: Expressions of Cause and Effect

   1. See the General Teaching Tips, page 11, for suggestions on teaching this section.

   2. Spend time going over the synonyms, e.g., *cause, lead to, result in*. Provide additional examples, and try to elicit examples from the students.

④ ANSWERS

       effect   causes

   2. Her success as a dancer <u>is the result of</u> hard work, good luck, and knowing the right people.

         cause   effect

   3. The love of money <u>is the root of</u> all evil. (Source: *The Bible, The New Testament*)

             cause

   4. Over 80 percent of the residents of the area are immigrants. <u>Therefore</u>, most

         effect

   children starting school do not speak English as their first language.

          effect   cause

   5. In some cities, homelessness <u>is a manifestation of</u> very high housing costs.

                    effect

   6. The parents were relieved to learn that their daughter's reading problem <u>was</u>

             cause

   <u>caused by</u> nothing worse than weak eyesight.

cause   effects

7. <u>Because of</u> poor sanitation, there were frequent outbreaks of cholera, dysentery, and typhoid fever in the refugee camp.

cause   effect

8. <u>If</u> children are not given sufficient love and affection as babies, they are likely to have difficulty forming close, trusting relationships as they grow up.

⑤ ANSWERS

1. result of
2. so, therefore
3. a manifestation of, is caused by
4. because

Taking Notes

1. See the General Teaching Tips, page 12, for suggestions on teaching this section.
2. In Exercise 6, follow the directions in the book precisely. Students should take notes on their own paper. Afterward, they should edit and rewrite their notes in the book.

⑥ SAMPLE OUTLINE

topic		**TWO CAUSES OF CRIME**
1st theory		I. Structural-functionist perspective
causes of crime	◯	A. ↑ crime result of
		· social disorg.
		· loss of shared values & norms
		· erosion of social control
origin of theory		B. Based on ideas of Thomas Merton, sociologist
		C. If theory is correct → crime will occur when
		there's rapid social change, e.g.,
examples of social change		· immigration
		· industrialization
		· increased poverty

(*continued*)

example–country	D. Canada
where is crime? reason	⭘ • murders ‹ in east than in west
	• east: more settled, people share sim. cult. →
	less crime
	• west: still migration, so less organized, less
	shared values → more crime
	• same in U.S.
other countries	E. Other countries
examples	• homogeneous, e.g., Japan, Korea → less crime
	• soc. changing rapidly, e.g., So. Africa → more crime
1st theory – conclusion	F. Struc-func = good theory for understanding
	causes of crime
2nd theory	⭘ II. Conflict theory
origin	A. Based on ideas of Karl Marx
cause of crime	B. Conflict between social classes ↑ crime, i.e., crime →
	inequality
	C. Laws created by people w/ power → protect their interests
examples	• e.g., property rights—help rich, not poor
	• wealthy people influence legal system, get best
	legal advice
	D. Law treats diff. classes differently
examples	• Canada: 12% of prison pop. = aboriginals, but
	abor = 4% of pop.
	⭘ • U.S. 41% of prisoners on Death Row = black;
	blacks = 12% of pop.
2nd theory– conclusion	E. Conflict theory can help to explain crime.

Reviewing the Lecture

See the General Teaching Tips, page 13, for suggestions on conducting this activity.

C. REAL TALK: USE WHAT YOU'VE LEARNED (page 190)

See the General Teaching Tips, page 6, for suggestions on teaching this section.

Vocabulary Review

See the General Teaching Tips, page 6, for suggestions on conducting the vocabulary review.

ANSWERS

1. Sociologists	**6.** manifestation
2. perspective, disorganization	**7.** social constructs
3. norms, erosion	**8.** capital, property
4. migration	**9.** aboriginals
5. homogeneous	**10.** comprise, Death Row

Discussion

See the General Teaching Tips, page 6, for suggestions on conducting discussions.

TOEFL Practice

1. See the General Teaching Tips, page 14, for suggestions on conducting this activity.
2. Every student talk will be different, but a complete answer should include the following information:

   The structural-functional theory of crime says that crime is the result of social disorganization that occurs at times of high immigration, industrialization, and increased poverty. The conflict theory states that crime is the result of inequality between social classes. All the conditions included in these two definitions are occurring now in China. Large numbers of people are moving from the rural areas into the cities. This creates social disorganization. At the same time, China's residency program creates inequalities between the city dwellers and the new migrants. These conditions may explain the huge increase in crime.

CHAPTER 8

LIGHTS, CAMERA, ACTION!

Part One: In Person

Background

"Lights, camera, action!" are the words spoken by a film director to initiate the filming of a scene.

Art

1. The photo shows a director on a film set, surrounded by cameras and other equipment.
2. See the General Teaching Tips, page 3, for suggestions on presenting art.

A. PRELISTENING (page 193)

See the General Teaching Tips, page 3, for suggestions on conducting prelistening speaking activities.

Discussion

See the General Teaching Tips, page 6, for suggestions on conducting discussions.

Vocabulary Preview

See the General Teaching Tips, page 4, for suggestions on conducting the vocabulary preview.

B. LISTENING (page 194)

Main Ideas

See the General Teaching Tips, page 4, for suggestions on teaching the Main Ideas section.

❶ ANSWERS
   2, 4, 6, 7, 8

Details and Inferences

See the General Teaching Tips, page 4, for suggestions on teaching this section.

❷ ANSWERS
   1. a. She produced a short film in high school.
      b. She interned before college.
      c. She went to film school.
   2. a

   3. c
   4. spend a lot of time phoning and e-mailing

5.

Genre/Theme	Adjectives
1. family comedy	broad, fun, smart
2. teen boys and grief	dark, gritty
3. thriller	scary
4. relationship movie	urban
5. comedy	big, romantic, fun
6. action	topical

6. a. great stories

b. great characters

7. *Answers will vary but should include three of the following:*
- well organized
- good at multitasking
- remembering everything
- following up on everything
- being on top of every project
- working every day

Listening for Language

See the General Teaching Tips, page 5, for suggestions on teaching this section.

❸ ANSWERS

1. chance	**4.** in the right place at the right time	**7.** iffy
2. opportunity	**5.** take a shot	**8.** not putting all your eggs in
3. luck	**6.** guaranteed	one basket

CONVERSATION TOOLS

See the General Teaching Tips, page 6, for suggestions on teaching Conversation Tools.

❺ ANSWERS

1. e	**3.** d	**5.** c	**7.** a
2. c	**4.** b	**6.** a	

❻ ANSWERS

1. be in the right place at the right time

2. iffy

3. take a chance

4. miss out on

5. take a shot

6. put all my eggs in one basket

C. REAL TALK: USE WHAT YOU'VE LEARNED (page 199)

Vocabulary Review

1. See the General Teaching Tips, page 6, for suggestions on conducting the vocabulary review.
2. Be sure to circulate as students are talking. Note cases where students both correctly and incorrectly use the vocabulary being reviewed.

② SAMPLE ANSWERS

Answers will vary. For example:

1. My favorite movie is [*Monsters, Inc.*] I like it because [the animation is brilliant and the characters are incredibly funny].
2. Film genres include action, adventure, animated / anime, comedy, crime, documentary, drama, historical, horror, musical, romance, science fiction, thriller, war, westerns.
3. Most jobs these days require workers to multitask and juggle schedules, e.g., administrative, finance, medicine, teaching, restaurant work.
4. Answers will vary.
5. Answers will vary.

Research: Movie Industry Jobs

1. Assign jobs to students or allow them to pick what interests them.
2. Instruct students to do an Internet search for *movie crew glossary* or *glossary of movie jobs* (students should not use quotation marks when searching). Most of the jobs can be found in the online encyclopedia Wikipedia.

Part Two: On the Phone

Art

1. The opening photo shows a movie theater. The films showing are displayed outside on the marquee.
2. See the General Teaching Tips, page 3, for suggestions on presenting art.

A. PRELISTENING (page 200)

See the General Teaching Tips, page 3, for suggestions on conducting prelistening speaking activities.

Discussion

See the General Teaching Tips, page 6, for suggestions on conducting discussions.

CULTURE NOTE

For more information about the movie ratings system used in the United States, go to the website for the Motion Picture Association of America at http://www.mpaa.org/.

Vocabulary Preview

See the General Teaching Tips, page 4, for suggestions on conducting the vocabulary preview.

B. LISTENING (page 201)
Main Ideas

See the General Teaching Tips, page 4, for suggestions on teaching the Main Ideas section.

❶ ANSWERS

theater name	film ratings
theater location	film running times
movies currently showing	ticket prices
showtimes	parking information

Details and Inferences

See the General Teaching Tips, page 4, for suggestions on teaching this section.

❷ ANSWERS

1.

You are a / an . . .	You want to see . . .	Day / Time of day	Showtime	Ticket price
1. 21-year-old student	*Batman Begins*	Wednesday evening	6:40 P.M.	$8.50
2. 62-year-old man	*March of the Penguins*	Sunday bargain matinee	12:15 P.M.	$7.50
3. Adult woman	*Stealth*	Saturday late show	12:30 A.M.	$7.50
4. Adult woman	*Stealth*	Monday early evening	7 P.M.	$9.00
5. 10-year-old child	*March of the Penguins*	Friday late afternoon	4:40 P.M.	$8.00

2. 1. e   2. c   3. a   4. b,   d

3. a. T   c. F (You can meet the director on Friday and Saturday nights.)
  b. T   d. F (Seniors pay $8.00. Soldiers pay $8.50.)
             e. F (Prices are $5 on weekends and $3 on weekdays.)

Listening for Language

See the General Teaching Tips, page 5, for suggestions on teaching this section.

See the General Teaching Tips, page 5, for suggestions on teaching Focus on Sound.

④ **ANSWERS**

	Voiceless /θ/	Voiced /ð/
1. Thursday		✓
2. there	✓	
3. theater		✓
4. through		✓
5. either	✓	
6. thank you		✓
7. *Stealth*		✓
8. others	✓	
9. further	✓	
10. with		✓
11. three		✓
12. without		✓

C. REAL TALK: USE WHAT YOU'VE LEARNED (page 204)

Vocabulary Review

1. See the General Teaching Tips, page 6, for suggestions on conducting the vocabulary review.
2. Be sure to circulate as students are talking. Note cases where students both correctly and incorrectly use the vocabulary being reviewed.
3. Some items, e.g., "Q and A," are not found in Exercise 2. Instruct students to look at the script in those cases.

❷ **SAMPLE ANSWERS**

Answers will vary. For example:
There's a bargain matinee of *March of the Penguins* on Sunday at 12:15.
Stealth has a Saturday late show.
On Wednesday, *Batman Begins* screens at 6:40 P.M.
The Monday evening showtime for *Stealth* is 7 P.M.

Note: The following information is in the script only:
The 7:35 show of *The Edukators* will be followed by Q and A.
Batman Begins has a running time of 2 hours and 35 minutes.
The Edukators is in German with subtitles in English.

Movie Theater Phone Recording

See page 218 of the Student Book for both Student A's and Student B's information. Each student will fill in the other's information.

Part Three: On the Air

Art

See the General Teaching Tips, page 3, for suggestions on presenting art.

A. PRELISTENING (page 206)

1. Ask students how many have seen the movie *Pirates of the Caribbean*. Ask those students not to reveal details about the film. Give students time to read the plot summary, but do not provide additional information at this time.
2. See the General Teaching Tips, page 3, for suggestions on conducting prelistening speaking activities.

Discussion

1. See the General Teaching Tips, page 6, for suggestions on conducting discussions.
2. To view a trailer of the film, do an Internet search for *"Pirates of the Caribbean: The Curse of the Black Pearl" + trailer.*

Vocabulary Preview

See the General Teaching Tips, page 4, for suggestions on conducting the vocabulary preview.

B. LISTENING (page 207)
Main Ideas

1. See the General Teaching Tips, page 4, for suggestions on teaching the Main Ideas section.
2. Give students time to read the box of movie-related terminology. All these terms are used in the interview. They are for information only and do not appear in the chapter test.

ANSWERS

1. They loved it.
2. He thought it was second-rate.

3. a. The film is badly directed.
   b. It's badly acted.
   c. It is emotionally sterile.

Details and Inferences

See the General Teaching Tips, page 4, for suggestions on teaching this section.

ANSWERS

1. c	**4.** a	**7.** a, b, c
2. c	**5.** two hours and twenty minutes	**8.** c
3. d	**6.** a	

Listening for Language

See the General Teaching Tips, page 5, for suggestions on teaching this section.

CONVERSATION TOOLS

See the General Teaching Tips, page 6, for suggestions on teaching Conversation Tools.

④ **ANSWERS**

1. f	**3.** d	**5.** a	**7.** h
2. g	**4.** e	**6.** b	**8.** c

C. REAL TALK: USE WHAT YOU'VE LEARNED (page 210)

Vocabulary Review

1. See the General Teaching Tips, page 6, for suggestions on conducting the vocabulary review.
2. In Exercise 2, students should provide antonyms that fit the context of the listening. "Sterile," for example, has one meaning in a medical context and quite a different meaning in the context of the film.

② **SAMPLE ANSWERS**

Answers will vary. For example:

Part Three Adjectives	Antonyms
corrupt	pure, consistent
eccentric	ordinary, conventional, predictable
grating	soothing, comforting, pleasant
mishandled	well-handled, well-done
scrubbed	dirty, gritty
second-rate	first-rate, excellent, outstanding, superior
sterile	rich, imaginative, complex
unbearable	bearable, tolerable, enjoyable
unendurable	pleasant, enjoyable

Discussion

See the General Teaching Tips, page 6, for suggestions on conducting discussions.

Presentation: Film Review

See the General Teaching Tips, page 8, for suggestions on conducting oral reports and presentations.

Part Four: In Class

Background

The lecture in this section is about postproduction movie sound, that is, sound that is added or re-created once the filming of a movie is finished. For background, please do an Internet search for the terms *"movie sound," "movie sound effects,"* or *Foley*. An outstanding site is "The Art of Foley" at http://www.marblehead.net/foley/index.html. See also "How Movie Sound Works" at http://entertainment.howstuffworks.com/movie-sound.htm.

Art

1. The photo shows a Foley stage. A Foley stage is an environment where sounds that are part of a film are re-created by actors. A simple example would be the sound of someone wearing cowboy boots walking across a wood floor.
2. See the General Teaching Tips, page 3, for suggestions on presenting art.

A. PRELISTENING (page 212)

See the General Teaching Tips, page 10, for suggestions on conducting prelistening activities.

Activity

1. Follow the directions in the Student Book for steps 1–3.
2. For the discussion in step 4, follow the suggestions in the General Teaching Tips, page 6, for conducting discussions.

Vocabulary Preview

See the General Teaching Tips, page 4, for suggestions on conducting the vocabulary preview.

B. LISTENING AND NOTE-TAKING (page 213)

See the General Teaching Tips, page 10, for suggestions on teaching this section.

Lecture Language: Defining Technical Terms

See the General Teaching Tips, page 11, for suggestions on teaching this section.

❷ ANSWERS
1. Production sound is natural sound from the production; actors speaking; ambient sound in the environment.
2. ADR stands for Automated Dialogue Replacement. It means re-recording dialogue in a studio.
   Looping is the same thing as ADR.
3. Group ADR (or group looping) is when a troop of actors is brought in to re-record all the background characters in a movie.
4. Sound effects is the addition of sound not in the dialogue.

(continued)

5. A Foley artist is a performer who performs sounds.

6. "In synch" means the movie's sound is at the same time as the picture.

7. Source music is music that comes from something in a scene. It's part of the scene, not background.

8. A mixing stage is the place where the dialogue, music, and sound effects are mixed together into the final soundtrack for a movie.

Lecture Organization: Logical Division

See the General Teaching Tips, page 11, for suggestions on teaching this section.

4 ANSWERS

1. postproduction sound

2. a. looping or ADR; b. sound effects and Foley; c. music

3. Any of these note-taking methods will work.

Taking Notes

1. See the General Teaching Tips, page 12, for suggestions on teaching this section.

2. Because this is the last chapter in the book, no scaffolding for note-taking is provided. On the basis of Exercise 4, students should choose the note-taking method they prefer. They may also combine methods as they listen and take notes. In order to reinforce what students have learned throughout the book, make sure that they revise and rewrite their notes after the lecture. You can assign this as homework or have them do it in class. This could also serve as a "final exam" in note-taking.

topic	Post-production sound = sound for film, TV, commercials, and other media
	3 elements of post-prod. sound:
	• dialogue and looping or ADR
	• sound effects and Foley
	• music composition and music editorial
1st element	I. Dialogue & ADR
production sound	A. Production sound
definition	1. On set, microphones capture sound = "production" sound, e.g., actors speaking, ambient sounds
	2. Problem: prod. sound inconsistent
	3. Post prod. takes prod. sound and edits, smoothes it out
ADR	B. ADR
	1. Sometimes things in prod. soundtrack can't be saved, e.g., there are loud sounds, swear word, don't like how actor said a line
definition	2. In those cases actors need to go into studio & replace dialogue = ADR = automated dialogue replacement = looping
definition	3. Group ADR = group looping: group of actors re-record. perf
	4. Reason: on set background actors must be silent; need to go back and fill in later

(continued)

2nd element	II. Sound effects & Foley
	A. Sound effects = any sound ↑ dialogue
◯	1. e.g., gunshot, car, dog barking
	2. physically cut / edit them into scenes
	B. Foley = unique way of recording sound
	1. watch picture & Foley artists perform sounds
	2. act out characters' movements
	3. e.g., clothes, footsteps, water (repetitive, hard
	to edit one sound at a time)
	4. Foley stage = audio environment w/ special
	floor, props
	5. process named after man named Foley
3rd element	III. Music
◯	A. Music composition
	1. composer watches video, dialogue, etc.
	2. composes music
	3. conducts orchestra & records in synch
	w/ picture
	4. can use synthesizers, electronic keyboards,
	or both
	B. Source music
	1. def: something in scene, not background
	2. e.g., music in bar, song on radio
final step	IV. Final step: Go to re-recording or "mixing" stage & mix
◯	dialogue, music, sound effects into final soundtrack
conclusion	V. Sound in film or TV show is almost 100% replaced.

Reviewing the Lecture

See the General Teaching Tips, page 13, for suggestions on conducting this activity.

C. REAL TALK: USE WHAT YOU'VE LEARNED (page 216)

See the General Teaching Tips, page 6, for suggestions on teaching this section.

Vocabulary Review

See the General Teaching Tips, pages 6, for suggestions on conducting the vocabulary review.

⊘ ANSWERS

1. F (Ambient sounds are called sound effects. Repetitive sounds are done by Foley artists.)
2. T
3. F (It is not in every movie.)
4. T
5. T
6. T
7. F (The soundtrack is produced on a re-recording or mixing stage.)
8. T
9. T
10. T

Project: Analyze a Soundtrack

1. A very short clip—two or three minutes at most—provides a sufficient amount to analyze. Action or adventure movies are probably easiest to analyze because they have many sound effects.
2. *Optional:* This activity can be done with the whole class.

TOEFL Practice

1. See the General Teaching Tips, page 14, for suggestions on conducting this activity.
2. Every student talk will be different, but a complete presentation should include the following information:

"Sound effects" means any kind of sound that is not dialogue and that is added to the soundtrack of a film during postproduction. Impact sounds like gunshots or ambient sounds like dogs barking are examples of sound effects. "Foley," in contrast, is a process in which performers act out the movements of the characters in the film and recreate the sounds produced by the actors' movements, such as the sound of clothes rubbing against each other or the sound of a person getting into a bathtub. Foley is different from sound effects because it must be acted out. For that reason it is done on a special stage. The two types of sound work together. Sound effects are used to create realistic background or environmental sounds. Foley is used to make the movements of the actors sound realistic.

CHAPTER
TESTS

INTRODUCTION TO CHAPTER TESTS

Each chapter of **Real Talk 2** is accompanied by a test that measures how well students have mastered the vocabulary, conversational phrases, idioms, and phonological features presented in the chapter. Tests are worth 40 points each.

TEST FEATURES

* a variety of tasks (fill-in-the-blank, open-ended questions, matching, etc.)
* answer keys and a scoring guide
* an audioscript for the listening sections

SUGGESTIONS FOR USE

Since the tests cover all the material in the chapter, we recommend using the tests in their entirety only if you have taught all four parts of the chapter. Otherwise, feel free to customize the tests and use only parts that are appropriate for your class.

The listening portions of the tests are not recorded; therefore, we have provided scripts for the instructors to read. We have also included pronunciation guidelines for stress, reductions, linking, and intonation. We recommend reading the items once, at a natural speed, and adhering to the guidelines provided. You may also want to ask a native speaker to record these listening sections.

CHAPTER **1**   **TEST**

A.   **Complete the sentences with a word or expression from the box. Change noun endings or verb forms if necessary. Not all words or expressions will be used. (10 points)**

adolescence	debt	minimize
anticipate	emerging	overreact
anxiety	euphoric	severe
bizarre	factor	stage
compromise (noun)	judgmental	stunned

1. "You want to eat out, I want to eat at home. Let's _____: We'll get take-out food and eat it at home."

2. People who are _____ and rigid are likely to suffer from culture shock more than people who are open-minded and flexible.

3. One way to _____ the effects of culture shock is to develop a support system in your new culture.

4. In Western cultures, _____ is usually defined as the period of time between the ages of thirteen and nineteen or twenty.

5. People suffering from culture shock often _____ to small annoyances. For example, they may start crying unexpectedly if someone pushes them on a train or bus.

6. I read a newspaper story about a _____ accident. A man driving on the highway was injured when a flying cow hit his car. (The cow had fallen out of a truck going in the opposite direction.)

7. Rachel felt _____ when she got the job of her dreams right after graduating from college. She bought a bottle of champagne to celebrate.

8. Andrew finished medical school with a _____ of $175,000.

9. Typically, the cultural adjustment cycle has four _____: the honeymoon period, culture shock, gradual adjustment, and adaptation.

10. I was _____ to hear that my neighbor, a quiet, elderly woman, won $11 million in the lottery.

B. **Complete the sentences with a word or expression from the box. Change noun endings or verb forms if necessary. Not all words or expressions will be used. (10 points)**

come about	give notice (at work)	out of the blue
come into contact	in retrospect	start out
entry level	land on one's feet	support system
get my act together	on the wrong track	switch gears

1. **A:** What do you enjoy most about your work as an English language teacher?

   B: Well, one thing I really like is the chance to _____ with people from different countries and cultures.

2. **A:** Why are you going back to school?

   B: Well, I've been working for my father for the past eight years. I feel like it's time to _____ and try something different.

3. **A:** Have you told your boss yet about your decision to leave the company?

   B: Yeah. I _____ last Thursday.

4. **A:** Does your new job give you health insurance?

   B: No. No insurance, no paid vacation, no pension. It's a(n) _____ job with no benefits. But I'm getting good experience, and I'm sure my next job will be better.

5. **A:** How did you become a writer?

   B: Well, I _____ as a teacher, and then I discovered I really love writing stories for kids.

6. **A:** I heard you moved back in with your parents.

   B: Yeah. I lost my job.

   A: How long do you plan to stay there?

   B: Just until I _____, you know, find another job and save some money.

7. **A:** Your mother said you got an acting role in a play!

   B: Yeah, that's right.

   A: How did that _____?

   B: Well, I auditioned for a small part in a different play last year, but they never called me back. I was thinking I should forget about acting and get a job in a bank or something, but then, _____, I got a call asking me to come audition for this new role. And I got it!

8. A: You're going to Italy to study for a year?

    B: Yeah. I'm really excited.

    A: Aren't you worried about being alone in a foreign country?

    B: Not at all. I have lots of relatives in Italy. I'm going to have a great _____ there.

9. A: How long have you been a lawyer?

    B: Thirty years.

    A: You must enjoy your work.

    B: No, actually I don't. _____, I wished I had become a university professor.

C. Your teacher will read the following sentences out loud. Underlined words are stressed. Listen and circle eight more stressed words. (4 points)

1. <u>After</u> I graduate, I'd <u>like</u> to <u>travel</u> in Africa for a <u>year</u>.

2. George was <u>depressed</u> for <u>months</u> after his company <u>transferred</u> him to Washington.

3. That's the most amazing <u>thing</u> I ever <u>heard</u>.

D. In the sentences below, find five pairs of linked or blended words. Draw an arc under the words to connect them. (5 points)

    EXAMPLE: talk about

1. How many twentysomethings do you know who still live at home?

2. There's no magical moment when a child becomes an adult.

E. Circle the pronunciation of the past tense verbs below. (5 points)

1. t   d   əd   changed

2. t   d   əd   regretted

3. t   d   əd   switched

4. t   d   əd   showed

5. t   d   əd   realized

F. **Complete the dialogues with expressions for giving and responding to good or bad news, as indicated in parentheses. (8 points)**

1. Man: (good news) _____. I asked my girlfriend to marry me, and she said yes!

   Friend: (respond to good news) _____. When's the wedding?

2. A: How do you like your new house?

   B: Well, it has lots of space, a new kitchen, and a huge backyard with a pool.

   A: It sounds great.

   B: It is, but (bad news) _____, it's really far from work. I have to drive forty-five minutes each way.

   A: (respond to bad news) _____.

G. **Write a short (four to five sentences) paragraph about a real or imagined turning point in your life. Use four of the words or expressions from the box. You may change verb or noun forms. (8 points)**

adjust(ment)	regret
change my mind	start out
in retrospect	supportive
make up my mind	

NAME _____

CHAPTER 2 TEST

A. Complete the sentences with a word or expression from the box. Change noun endings or verb forms if necessary. Not all words or expressions will be used. (15 points)

accommodate	idiomatic	pick up
brainstorm	in the habit	rehearse
easier said than done	on the fence	session
fit in	option	smog
have an ear	pet peeve	tailored

1. While living in Paris, I got _____ of stopping at the corner café for an espresso on my way to work every morning.

2. People who _____ for languages are usually able to acquire good pronunciation in any language they learn.

3. This language course is _____ to people who work in the hotel business.

4. One of my _____ is people who talk on cell phones in restaurants. I think that is really rude.

5. The dance class costs $450 for a ten-week _____.

6. The lecture hall was designed to comfortably _____ only 300 people, yet 500 squeezed in to hear the famous author speak about his latest book.

7. Janet and Daniel have been going out for two years. She wants to get married soon, but he is _____. He wants to save more money before getting married.

8. Her literary German is excellent, but she is not familiar with the _____ language.

9. The managers spent three days _____ about ways to increase profits and avoid laying off employees.

10. "The play opens on September 1. Until then we will _____ three times a week. Act 1 lines should be memorized by next Thursday," the director said.

11. Cooking Mexican food is _____. The ingredients are simple, but knowing how to combine them and which spices to use is tricky.

12. _____ levels were so high in Los Angeles last week that sensitive people were warned to stay indoors.

13. You can choose one of three _____ for getting to San Francisco: drive, fly, or take the train.

14. The most important thing in a teenager's life is _____ with his or her classmates. As one teen put it, "My friends are my life."

15. Irina _____ English by working in a factory. She never attended a language school.

B. Complete each short dialogue with a different expression for restating or asking for clarification. (4 points)

1. Teacher: I'm going to give you a little rhyme to help you remember how to spell certain words. Ready? "When the sound is "ee", it's *i* before *e*, except after *c*."

Pupil: _____. It's / it's *i* before *e* in words like *field*, but it's *e* before *i* in *receive*, for example.

Teacher: That's right.

2. Teacher: The requirements for the course are weekly quizzes, a reading journal, a midterm exam or a five-page paper, and a final.

Student: _____ a midterm and a five-page paper?

Teacher: No, a midterm *or* a five-page paper.

C. Complete each short excerpt with a different expression that signals the main idea. (4 points)

1. Teacher: (to student) I asked you to come talk to me because you've been late to class every day this week. And, let's see, you got a D minus on the last exam, and you didn't turn in the essay that was due on Tuesday. _____, you're going to fail this course if you don't get serious and start working.

2. Doctor: I have patients who work out religiously. They're at the gym for hours every week. But how do they get to the gym? They drive. And then they drive home. And they drive to the grocery store three blocks away. They pay someone to wash their car, to walk their dog, to clean their house, to take care of their garden. _____, if these people would walk or ride a bicycle or do their own housework, they wouldn't need to belong to a gym!

D. Your teacher will read the following sentences. Listen to the intonation at the end of the sentence. Draw a rising ↗, falling ↘, or flat → arrow to indicate the intonation you hear. (5 points)

_____ **1.** I couldn't go back to the country I had come from.

_____ **2.** I didn't do any formal training or any formal studies.

_____ **3.** I made flash cards to remember vocabulary.

_____ **4.** I would start conversations with people in the grocery store.

_____ **5.** I read comic books in English.

E. Your teacher will read the following sentences. Listen and insert slashes (/) between thought groups. Do not insert slashes at the ends of sentences. (5 points)

1. She works in the university library from 3 to 6 P.M. Tuesday to Sunday.

2. I have no idea where my daughter went or who she's with.

3. The boy's shoes are too small and his pants are too short.

F. Your teacher will read the following sentences. Underline seven stressed words. (7 points)

A: I got a ticket today.

B: What for?

A: I forgot to put money in the parking meter.

B: That's a shame.

G. The box lists cohesive devices. Write the letter of one of the devices next to each numbered item in the lecture excerpt. Some items may have more than one correct answer, but you should only write one letter. You will not use all the devices. (4 points)

a. repetition of keywords	c. use of words from the	d. pronoun reference
b. use of synonym	same family	e. transitions

Now, in English, the main mechanism we have for creating new words is a process called _derivation_, which means we create—or we _derive_ (1. _____)—new words from existing <u>ones</u> (2. _____) by adding prefixes or suffixes to them. Uh, so <u>for example</u> (3. _____), we can take the word, the root "use," u-s-e, and by adding prefixes and suffixes we get _useful, useless, misuse, unusable, abuse,_ and so on. So that's an example of <u>derivation</u> (4. _____).

H. Write a short paragraph (three to four sentences) in response to this question: Are you a "formal" English learner, a "natural" learner, or both? Give at least three reasons or examples to support your answer. (6 points)

_____

_____

_____

_____

_____

_____

CHAPTER 3 TEST

A. Your teacher will read several questions. Listen and circle whether the final intonation is rising ↗ or falling ↘. (4 points)

1. rising   falling

2. rising   falling

3. rising   falling

4. rising   falling

B. The following sentences have some stressed words underlined. Listen and circle eight additional stressed words. (4 points)

1. It'll take <u>three years</u> to pay back my student loans.

2. There's <u>no</u> service charge if you keep a minimum balance of <u>two hundred</u> and <u>fifty dollars</u>.

3. We're <u>going</u> broke. It's <u>time</u> to cut down on <u>extras</u>.

C. Listen to a short passage about credit card debt in the United States. It will be read twice. Take notes in the space. (10 points)

_____

_____

_____

_____

D. Read these sentences taken from news stories. Replace the underlined words with synonyms. (4 points)

1. Statistics show that from 2000 until 2005, the average price of a home in New York City <u>increased</u> from nearly $251,000 to $449,000—a(n) <u>increase</u> of 79 percent.

2. Japan's Sharp Corp., the world's biggest maker of solar cells, expects the cost of generating solar power to <u>decrease by 50 percent</u> by 2010.

3. Sales of Ford and General Motors trucks and SUVS have <u>decreased</u> significantly as a direct result of sky-high gasoline prices.

E. **Complete the sentences with a word or expression from the box. Change noun endings or verb forms if necessary. Not all words or expressions will be used. (10 points)**

appropriate	cut corners	itemize
balance	cut out	laid off
coupon	deadline	make ends meet
cut back	double	waive

1. In the United States, the _____ for paying income taxes is April 15 of each year. You must pay your taxes by that date or pay a fine.

2. Normally there is a $5 fee for opening a checking account. However, that fee is _____ if you open a savings account at the same time.

3. The first thing you must do when planning a budget is to _____ all your expenses. If your expenses are greater than your income, then it is time to _____ on your spending.

4. After paying all my bills last month, my bank _____ was $230.

5. One way to save money is to use discount _____ at the grocery store.

6. After George was _____ from his third job in three years, he found it necessary to borrow money from his parents. It was the only way he was able to _____.

7. Interest rates have _____ from 2 percent to 4 percent in less than a year.

8. In American culture it is not _____ to ask people how much money they make.

F. **Complete the sentences with a word or expression from the box. Change noun endings or verb forms if necessary. Not all words or expressions will be used. (10 points)**

accumulate	get by	live within one's means
come up short	grant	pay back
end up	impact	pay off
garage sale	kiss off	segment

1. Alfonso received a $15,000 _____ to attend Harvard University.

2. My brother-in-law still has not _____ the money I lent him more than four years ago. I guess it's time to _____ that money and stop hoping he'll repay it.

3. Winning a million dollars in the lottery did not have a huge _____ on Mr. Gregory's life. He still lives in the same house, drives the same car, and goes to work every day.

4. The only way that many young adults can _____ is to live at home or rent an apartment with roommates.

5. The poorest _____ of the U.S. population consists of immigrants who have little education and do not speak English.

6. Next month, we will _____ our car loan, and then we plan to start saving money for a trip to China.

7. Sandra _____ on very little sleep. That's how she manages to work and go to school full time.

8. No matter how careful I am with my money, I always seem to _____ at the end of the month. Maybe it's time to get a better job.

9. Believe it or not, I bought this cashmere sweater at a _____.

G. **Write a short paragraph in response to this question: Would you lend money to a relative? Why or why not? Use at least four of the following words:** *borrow, lend, loan, pay back, debt, interest, do without.* **(8 points)**

_____

_____

_____

_____

_____

_____

CHAPTER 4 TEST

A. **Your teacher will say the answers to the questions below. Listen carefully to the sentence stress and write the letter of each answer next to its matching question. (5 points)**

_____ 1. Where did Robert lose his cell phone?

_____ 2. What did Robert lose?

_____ 3. Who lost his cell phone on the bus?

_____ 4. What did Robert do with his cell phone?

_____ 5. When did Robert lose his cell phone?

B. **Complete the sentences with different expressions for apologizing, reconciling, and forgiving, as indicated. (10 points)**

1. **A:** It was my birthday yesterday, you know.

    B: Oh no! I forgot! I had such a crazy day yesterday, I forgot to check the calendar. (apologizing) _____.

    A: (forgiving) _____, really.

    B: No, listen. (reconciling) _____. I'll take you to lunch Friday, OK?

    A: It's a deal.

2. **A:** (apologizing) _____ for shouting. I was really angry.

    B: (forgiving) _____.

C. **Complete the sentences with phrases that signal hypothetical situations. Use a different phrase each time. (4 points)**

1. _____ you forgot to bring your English homework to school on the day it was due. What would you do?

2. _____ that you are a vegetarian. A good friend invites you to dinner and serves meat as the main course. Would you eat it?

3. _____ you were the teacher in this class, and you caught several students cheating on the midterm exam? How would you handle it?

4. _____ that you arrive at a theater to see a play and you find another person sitting in your seat. You compare tickets, and they are the same! What would you do?

D. From the following group of words, pick out five pairs of synonyms and write them on the lines. (5 points)

bring back	extend	picture	transform
elaborate	modify	recall	trigger
evocative	phase	stage	visualize

1. _____

2. _____

3. _____

4. _____

5. _____

E. Complete the sentences with a word or expression from the box. Change noun endings or verb forms if necessary. Not all words or expressions will be used. (10 points)

absentmindedness	mind's eye	scatterbrain
enhance	on one's mind	sequence
evocative	procedure	slip one's mind
facilitate	recode	systematic
		the end of the world

1. In the following _____, can you figure out which number comes next: 2, 4, 7, 11, 16?

2. **A:** Did you remember to pick up the dry cleaning?

   B: Oops. It _____. I'll get it tomorrow on the way home from work.

3. I'm worried about my seventy-five-year-old father's _____. Last week, he forgot two doctor's appointments, and the other day, he couldn't remember where he parked his car.

4. Saying new words out loud is one way to _____ remembering them.

5. **A:** Do you have something _____? You've been very quiet this evening.

   B: No, it's nothing. I'm just tired.

6. The neighborhood where I grew up is gone now, but in my
_____, I can picture the way it used to be, with pretty little
houses and children playing everywhere.

7. The smell of chicken soup is _____ of my grandmother's
kitchen. I used to sit and talk to her while she was cooking.

8. **A:** Oh no! I locked my keys in the car!

   B: It's not _____. I have a spare set in my purse.

9. **A:** It's 8 A.M.! I'm going to be late for work!

   B: It's Saturday, you _____! Go back to sleep.

10. Mnemonics are _____ strategies for helping us remember
information that is hard to recall.

F. **Which of the following are examples of ways to recode information, according to Dr. Mel Levine? Check three correct answers. (3 points)**

_____ **a.** think of examples of it

_____ **b.** say it in another language

_____ **c.** describe it in words

_____ **d.** repeat it over and over

_____ **e.** memorize it

_____ **f.** make a picture of it

G. **Complete the following metaphor with your own idea and explain your answer in two to three sentences. (4 points)**

Memory is like a _____ _____

_____

_____

_____

_____

H. Write two to three sentences about a sensory memory of yours and what triggers or triggered it. (3 points)

_____

_____

_____

_____

_____

I. Show your understanding of the keyword method. Choose a word from your first language, give its English definition, and explain how you would use the keyword method to help your teacher learn this word. (6 points)

_____

_____

_____

_____

_____

CHAPTER 5 TEST

A. Your teacher will read sentences containing the sets of items below. As you hear each item, draw a rising ↗ or falling ↘ arrow above it to show the intonation you heard. (6 points)

1. plane   train   car

2. water   juice   soda

B. Complete the short conversations with different expressions of support or understanding. (4 points)

1. Teenager: It isn't fair that I have to be home by midnight when all my friends get to stay out as late as they want.

    Parent: Jeffrey, _____. But we think midnight is late enough for a fifteen-year-old. When you turn sixteen, we can talk about letting you stay out later.

2. A: I think we need some new political leadership in this state. This governor hasn't accomplished anything in the past four years.

    B: _____. I plan to vote for the other party in the next election.

C. Complete the statements with different expressions that signal generalizations. (6 points)

1. Dogs are social animals that, _____, should not be left alone for long periods of time.

2. Travelers to Bangkok can expect warm but rainy weather _____.

3. _____, the lectures in this course have been interesting.

D. Fill in the blanks with different strong, neutral, or weak expressions that mean "yes." (5 points)

1. A: Do you believe that you look younger since you had plastic surgery?

    B: Oh, _____. (strong)

2. A: Do you think the president's economic policies are helping to create more jobs?

    B: Well, _____. (weak)

3. A: You're sure you remembered to lock the door?

   B: _____. (strong)

4. A: Do you think this color looks good on me?

   B: _____. (neutral) It matches your green eyes.

5. A: Do you think the price of gasoline is going to come down anytime soon?

   B: _____. (weak) But of course no one knows for sure.

E. Read the excerpts from a research report. In each blank space, write the letter of the section the passage probably came from. (5 points)

I = introduction   M = methods   R = results   D = discussion

_____ **1.** In the body image study, the Taiwanese men exhibited significantly less body dissatisfaction than their Western counterparts.

_____ **2.** Men in Taiwan society appear less preoccupied with male body image than men in Western societies. This difference may reflect 1) Western traditions emphasizing muscularity and fitness as measures of masculinity . . .

_____ **3.** The authors hypothesized that Taiwanese men would exhibit less dissatisfaction with their bodies than Western men.

_____ **4.** The authors administered a computerized test of body image to fifty-five heterosexual men in Taiwan and compared the results to those previously obtained in an identical study in the United States and Europe.

_____ **5.** Previous studies by the authors have shown that young Western men display unrealistic body ideals and that Western advertising seems to place an increasing value on the male body.

F. Fill in the blanks with expressions of contrast. Pay attention to grammar and punctuation. (4 points)

1. In Taiwanese women's magazines, advertising portrayed Western-looking men wearing little or no clothing about 43 percent of the time, _____ the rate for Asian men was only 5 percent. It appears, therefore, that the Taiwanese place less emphasis on muscularity in men than do Western cultures.

2. Over the last several decades, disorders of body image have grown increasingly common among men in Western societies. . . . This _____ findings in non-Western societies, where male body image disorders appear to be rare.

Source: "Male Body Image in Taiwan Versus the West: *Yanggang Zhiqi* Meets the Adonis Complex," Chi-Fu Jeffrey Yang; Peter Gray, Ph.D.; and Harrison G. Pope Jr., M.D., M.P.H. http://ajp.psychiatryonline.org/cgi/content/full/162/2/263.

3. Western societies since ancient times have seen fitness and muscularity as measures of masculinity, as illustrated by Greek and Roman statues or the heroes of mythology. _____, there does not seem to be a comparable historical focus on male muscularity in China.

4. [In an experiment using drawings of male figures,] American college men chose an ideal body image far more muscular than themselves and also estimated that women prefer a very muscular male body. Actual college women, _____, did not prefer a male figure with large muscles.

G. **Complete the sentences with a word or expression from the box. Change noun endings or verb forms if necessary. Not all words or expressions will be used. (10 points)**

a hard time	fired up	regret
account (verb)	fit in	self-esteem
boost	in great shape	think (something) through
distorted	in short	washed out

1. Healthy _____ is based on people's ability to see themselves accurately and to accept and value themselves regardless of their weaknesses.

2. What do you think _____ for the boss's bad mood lately? Is the company in trouble?

3. I don't look good in the color white. With my blond hair, it makes me look _____.

4. Gail has a _____ idea about the size of her nose. In reality, it is not large.

5. Fresh from law school, Benjamin was all _____ about his first job and enthusiastically accepted every task he was given.

6. **A:** I'm planning to drive across the United States next December.

    B: In the middle of winter? Have you _____ this plan _____? It's not going to be much fun driving through rain and snow in that old car of yours.

7. **A:** How's your mom doing?

    B: She's not _____. Since the accident, she's been in a lot of pain.

8. **A:** Why did Jeremy come home early from summer camp?

    B: He says he was homesick, and he didn't _____ with the other kids.

9. **A:** Why should I take vitamins?

    B: You don't eat enough fruits or vegetables. Vitamins can _____ your energy level and make you feel stronger.

10. A: I want you to clean up your room. Hang up those clothes and put away your CDs.

   B: Mom, please don't give me _____. I promise to do that stuff this weekend. Right now I have too much homework.

H. **Complete the sentences with a word or expression from the box. Change noun endings or verb forms if necessary. Not all words or expressions will be used. (10 points)**

analyze	disorder	get tired
bulked up	for a change	handwriting is on the wall
bump	for one thing	on (one's) own
conduct	get ahead	run . . . by

1. I'm _____ a survey about people's use of cell phones. Would you have a few minutes to answer a few questions?

2. In certain industries, it is advantageous to look young if a person wants to

   _____.

3. I need to _____ this research idea _____ my professor. I'm not sure how practical it is.

4. I hadn't seen my classmate Josh for two years until I ran into him at a party last night. I couldn't believe my eyes—he had gotten so _____! He was huge!

5. David and Donna worked hard, saved their money, and bought a house in a good neighborhood _____, with no help from their families.

6. It is estimated that as many as 1 out of 10 teenage girls suffers from an eating _____ such as anorexia or bulimia.

7. These statistics don't look right to me. I think you need to _____ the data again.

8. **A:** How'd you get that huge _____ on your forehead?

   B: I hit my head on an open cabinet door.

9. **A:** What are you doing?

   B: Typing up my resumé. The _____ at my company. It's time to start job-hunting.

10. **A:** Want to go out to club tonight?

    B: No, thanks. I'm going to stay home _____ and go to bed early.

CHAPTER **6** TEST

A. **Read the information below about recent scientific discoveries. Then listen as your teacher reads sentences with modals and fill in the blanks. Use conventional spelling. (10 points)**

Cassini-Huygens is the name of a space mission intended to study the planet Saturn. Its spacecraft entered into orbit around Saturn on July 1, 2004, and has been sending back photographs and scientific information since then. One question scientists are investigating is how Saturn got its rings. One theory is that a meteor _____ one of

1

Saturn's moons and shattered it into tiny pieces that began orbiting the planet independently. Scientists never _____ this discovery without the use of

2

high-powered telescopes positioned on the spacecraft.

Meanwhile, here on Earth, astronomers are doing research on planets that _____ habitable. Using computer models, the scientists have calculated the

3

existence of at least 200 planets that _____ liquid water and an

4

atmosphere—conditions considered necessary for life.

In August of 2006, archaeologists in China discovered dinosaur fossils similar to ones found earlier in North America. The discovery raises the possibility that millions of years ago, Asia and North America _____ connected.

5

B. **Listen as your teacher reads sentences with reduced forms and syllable deletion. Fill in the blanks with the missing words. Use conventional spelling. (10 points)**

1. My new neighbors are _____ strange.

2. My husband's _____ loves to tell _____ stories about her family.

3. I'm _____ have a piece _____ chocolate.

4. Sorry, I _____ hear your _____.

5. I _____ come to your party, but I couldn't find a ride.

6. I _____ when they _____ for the airport.

C. Read the urban legends below and respond with a different expression of skepticism each time. (After the test, your teacher will tell you if the statements are true or false.) (6 points)

1. **A:** People driving red cars receive more traffic tickets for speeding than people driving cars of other colors.

   B: _____

2. **A:** It takes more calories to eat a piece of celery than the celery has in it to begin with.

   B: _____

3. **A:** You should wait at least an hour after eating before you go swimming. Otherwise you can get a stomach cramp and drown.

   B: _____

D. Fill in the blanks with different expressions for digressing and returning to the topic. (3 points)

A: What did you do on Saturday?

B: My wife and I decided we'd start cleaning out the garage. You wouldn't believe how much junk we've collected in there. There are boxes from my grandmother's attic, not to mention all the garden tools, bicyles, camping equipment . . .

   _____, we decided it was time to start going through it all. . . .

   ₁

A: I should do the same thing. It's been years since we've been able to put a car in our garage.

B: Yeah, well, _____, I opened this one box and you wouldn't

   ₂

   believe what I found in there. Letters written by my great-great-grandfather during the Civil War!

A: No kidding. Those must be worth a lot of money. You might be able to sell them on the Internet.

B: Maybe; I don't know. But _____, what I wanted to say was,

   ₃

   we spent three hours reading the letters instead of cleaning out the garage.

E. **Read the assertion and three pieces of supporting proof. Rewrite each proof statement and add an expression for providing proof. (9 points)**

    Assertion: The Earth is becoming gradually warmer.

    Proof:

1. Sea temperatures have risen 0.5° C over the past forty years.

    _____

    _____

2. A team led by Ruth Curry of Woods Hole Oceanographic Institution in Massachusetts has established that 20,000 square kilometers of freshwater ice melted in the Arctic between 1965 and 1995.[1]

    _____

    _____

3. Scientists have announced that a vast frozen area in Western Siberia is undergoing its first thaw since the end of the Ice Age, 11,000 years ago.[2]

    _____

    _____

F. **Complete the sentences with a word or expression from the box. Change noun endings or verb forms if necessary. Not all words or expressions will be used. (12 points)**

appraise	fake	obsession
commodities	funding	resist
conducive	give (someone) credit	run of the mill
distinctive	gut feeling	sharp as a tack
drop in the bucket	initiate	site

1. The amount of money that's spent on education is a _____ compared to the amount that's spent on weapons.

2. **A:** How did you find the restaurant without an address or directions?

    B: Oh, I just had a _____ about it.

3. You can recognize people from Boston by the _____ way they pronounce the letter "r" in words like "car."

[1] http://www.timesonline.co.uk/article/0,,3-1489955,00.html
[2] http://www.abc.net.au/worldtoday/content/2005/s1436206.htm

4. A: How much is that necklace worth?

   B: I have no idea. It's never been _____.

5. Switzerland's most famous _____ include electronics, watches, and chocolate.

6. A growing _____ with death led Silvia to begin psychiatric treatment.

7. This is the _____ where the dinosaur skeleton was discovered.

8. Her earrings are _____, but they look like real diamonds.

9. At age 100, Mrs. Franks is still as _____.

10. The university president spends a lot of time trying to get _____ for a new school of engineering.

11. A: How's that book you started reading last weekend?

   B: It's nothing special, just a _____ love story.

12. At age twenty-five, Agnes was extremely shy and almost never _____ conversations with men.

CHAPTER 7 TEST

A. Read the following situations and respond with sentences containing different expressions of sympathy. (6 points)

1. **A:** My grandmother broke her hip, and now she has to use a wheelchair.

   B: _____

2. **A:** Did you see that homeless guy going through the trash, looking for stuff to recycle?

   B: _____

3. **A:** I'm totally in shock. My parents just told me they're getting a divorce—after thirty-four years of marriage!

   B: _____

B. Listen to phrases with linking. Write the phrases. (4 points)

1. _____

2. _____

3. _____

4. _____

C. In the sets of words below, stressed syllables are shown in capital letters. Circle the letter of the word in each set that has correct stress. (5 points)

1. a. Economic   b. eCONomic   c. ecoNOMic   d. econoMIC

2. a. GOVernment   b. goVERNment   c. governMENT

3. a. PORtuguese   b. portuGUESE   c. porTUguese

4. a. comFORTable   b. COMfortable   c. comforTAble   d. comfortaBLE

5. a. oRIGinality   b. origiNALity   c. Originality   d. originalITY

D. Using the information below, write complete sentences that include the topic, your first impression of the topic, and your second thoughts. (Use your imagination if necessary.) Add your own words as needed. (6 points)

Topic	First impression	Second thought
1. history professor	strict, demanding	excellent teacher—treated us like adults
2. buy a car	convenient	hard to find parking gas is expensive

1. _____

   _____

2. _____

   _____

E. Write sentences using the cause and effect given below. Use a different expression of cause or effect each time. You may change the forms of words. Use past tense. (8 points)

Cause: Requiring gun owners to take a gun-safety course

Effect: A reduction in the number of gun-related accidents

1. _____

   _____

2. _____

   _____

3. _____

   _____

4. _____

   _____

F. Match the people in the left column with their descriptions on the right. Write the letters of the descriptions in the blank spaces. (5 points)

_____ 1. defendant

_____ 2. prosecutor

_____ 3. witness

_____ 4. jury

_____ 5. suspect

a. in a court of law, a group of people whose job is to determine if a person accused of a crime is guilty or innocent

b. in court, the person accused of a crime

c. an attorney whose job is to represent the state against a person accused of a crime

d. the person chosen to be the head of a jury

e. a police officer whose job is to solve crimes

f. a person arrested by the police on suspicion of having committed a crime

g. someone who has been targeted by a criminal act

h. a person who sees a crime committed

G. Complete the sentences with a word or expression from the box. Change noun endings or verb forms if necessary. Not all words or expressions will be used. (10 points)

assault	end up	generate	speed
deliberate	erode	infuriate	testify
empower	evidence	make	violation

1. The jury _____ for three days before returning a verdict of "not guilty."

2. When politicians lie or steal, their actions _____ the public's trust in the democratic process.

3. The judge dismissed the case against the suspected robber because there was not

   enough _____ to prove that he committed the crime.

4. My sister dropped out of high school and _____ selling shoes at a shop in the mall.

5. Residents of my street were _____ when one of the neighbors drove his motorcycle up and down the street at 60 miles per hour.

6. It is a _____ of the law to dump garbage in an alley behind people's houses.

7. The witness to the car accident could not remember the color or the

_____ of the car.

8. Three police officers _____ for the prosecution in the trial of a woman accused of selling drugs to college students.

9. Jordan's excellent marks in English _____ him to apply for a summer job as an intern at a newspaper.

10. The downtown construction project will _____ about 400 new jobs.

H. Imagine that you live in a large city where there are panhandlers in the downtown business district. Should panhandling be allowed, or should legal action be taken to either ban or limit it? State your opinion in three to four sentences. Use at least three of the following words: *menacing, ordinance, arrest, keep someone away from somewhere, threaten.* (6 points)

_____

_____

_____

_____

CHAPTER 8 TEST

A. Your teacher will read some phrases. Listen for whether they contain a voiced or voiceless *th*. Check (✓) the proper column to indicate the sound you heard. (5 points)

	Voiceless /θ/	Voiced /ð/
1.		
2.		
3.		
4.		
5.		

B. Complete the following sentences from a movie review with terms from the box that have the opposite meaning of the underlined items. (5 points)

coherent	grating	second rate
eccentric	inconsistent	sterile
flop	mishandled	unbearably

1. *Snakes on a Plane*, which cost $35 million to make, brought in only $13 million on its opening weekend. A better name for the film would have been *Snakes on a <u>Great Success</u>*. _____

2. With a running time of 2 hours and 35 minutes, the film was <u>pleasantly</u> long.

   _____

3. The <u>comforting</u> soundtrack, consisting of random electronic "music" and painfully amplified sound effects, almost drove me out of the theater. _____

4. The performance by lead actor Samuel L. Jackson was <u>unified and even</u>, ranging from believable to ridiculous. _____

5. Every aspect of this movie—acting, directing, and production—was <u>well done</u>._____

C. **Write complete sentences using the terms and definitions in the box. Use a different definition signal or structure in each sentence. (8 points)**

Term	Definition
1. feature film	a full-length movie, usually about 90–120 minutes in length
2. film score	music for a movie or a television show
3. gaffer	the chief electrician, the person responsible for the lighting on a movie set
4. cartoon	an animated film that is not of feature length

1. _____

2. _____

3. _____

4. _____

D. **Tell a short anecdote using each of the idioms below. Write one to three complete sentences per item. Use the idiom in your story. (12 points)**

Tell about a time when . . .

1. you missed out on an opportunity: _____

   _____

   _____

2. you were in the right place at the right time: _____

   _____

   _____

3. you took a chance: _____

   _____

   _____

4. you had the time of your life: _____

   _____

   _____

E. Write the letter of the movie term next to its definition. (10 points)

_____ 1. thriller

_____ 2. matinee

_____ 3. screen (verb)

_____ 4. set

_____ 5. cast

_____ 6. rating

_____ 7. shoot

_____ 8. running time

_____ 9. subtitles

_____ 10. a short

a. the length of a movie

b. translations of movie dialogue into another language, which appears at the bottom of the screen

c. the interior or exterior location where the action of a movie takes place

d. P, PG, PG-17, R, etc.

e. a movie that is less than forty-five minutes long

f. the group of actors appearing in a movie

g. a midday showing of a film

h. a film with an exciting plot involving crime, mystery, or suspense

i. film a movie

j. show a film for audiences to see

F. Complete the sentences with a word or expression from the box. Change noun endings or verb forms if necessary. Not all words or expressions will be used. (10 points)

ambient	iffy	Q and A
component	in synch	swear word
eccentric	juggle	take a shot
fall apart	multitask	topical

1. My chemistry teacher, Mr. Nathan, is a(n) _____ character. He is constantly telling jokes that nobody laughs at—except him!

2. The winning couple in the ice skating competition skated perfectly

   _____, almost as if they were one person.

3. A scientific study in which subjects were asked to switch between tasks revealed that

   _____ leads to more errors and less efficient use of time than

   performing one task at a time with one's full attention.

4. At the end of the lecture the speaker left fifteen minutes for _____.

5. A key scene of the film had to be reshot because the actor accidentally said

   a(n)_____.

6. The movie was about a relationship that begins promisingly but eventually

_____ when the woman finds out the man lied to her about his

family background.

7. There are three _____ to movie sound: dialogue, sound effects,
and music.

8. Our plans are _____ at the moment. If you call me tomorrow, I'll
be able to give you a definite answer.

9. The restaurant patio was a beautiful, relaxing place. The only _____
noise consisted of birds singing and people speaking quietly.

10. The math teacher asked who wanted to try to solve a complicated problem. I said I'd

_____ at it.

SCRIPTS FOR CHAPTER TESTS

Chapter Test 1, Part C

NOTE TO TEACHER: Please read items with natural speed and intonation. Be sure to enunciate the stressed words (underlined or circled) slightly louder, more clearly, and at a higher pitch than unstressed words, but do not exaggerate them.

1. After I graduate I'd like to travel in Africa for a year.

2. George was depressed for months after his company transferred him to Washington.

3. That's the most amazing thing I ever heard.

Chapter Test 2, Part D

NOTE TO TEACHER: Read the sentences with clear but natural rising and falling intonation, as indicated.

1. I couldn't go back to the country I had come from.

2. I didn't do any formal training or any formal studies.

3. I made flash cards to remember vocabulary.

4. I would start conversations with people in the grocery store.

5. I read comic books in English.

Chapter Test 2, Part E

NOTE TO TEACHER: Read at natural speed. Be sure to insert pauses naturally between thought groups as indicated by slashes.

1. She works in the university library / from three to six P.M. / Tuesday to Sunday.

2. I have no idea / where my daughter went / or who she's with.

3. The boy's shoes are too small / and his pants are too short.

Chapter Test 2, Part F

NOTE TO TEACHER: Please read items with natural speed and intonation. Be sure to enunciate the stressed words slightly louder, more clearly, and at a higher pitch than unstressed words, but do not exaggerate them.

> **A:** I got a TICKET today.
> **B:** What FOR?
> **A:** I FORGOT to put MONEY in the parking meter.
> **B:** THAT'S a SHAME.

Chapter Test 3, Part A

NOTE TO TEACHER: Read the sentences with clear but natural rising and falling intonation, as indicated.

> **1.** INTEREST rates are pretty LOW now, AREN'T THEY?
>
> **2.** Do you want to open a CHECKING ACCOUNT, a SAVINGS ACCOUNT, or BOTH?
>
> **3.** You spent HOW much on a new car?
>
> **4.** FOUR percent INTEREST ISN'T very HIGH, IS it?

Chapter Test 3, Part B

NOTE TO TEACHER: Please read items with natural speed and intonation. Be sure to enunciate the stressed words slightly louder, more clearly, and at a higher pitch than unstressed words, but do not exaggerate them.

> **1.** It'll take three years to pay BACK my STUDENT LOANS.
>
> **2.** There's no SERVICE charge if you keep a MINIMUM BALANCE of two hundred and fifty dollars.
>
> **3.** We're going BROKE. It's time to cut DOWN on extras.

Chapter Test 3, Part C

NOTE TO TEACHER: Read the text below at least twice. The first time, read it with no pauses and instruct students to listen without writing. The second time, pause after each sentence for students to write notes.

You have probably heard that the average American has more than $8,000 in credit card debt. Hower, this number is not exactly correct. In fact, 25 percent of American households have no credit cards at all. Another 31 percent pay off their credit card bills each month. In other words, 56 percent of American households actually have no credit card debt at all.

Chapter Test 4, Part A

a. ROBERT lost his cell phone on the bus this morning.

b. Robert LOST his cell phone on the bus this morning.

c. Robert lost his CELL PHONE on the bus this morning.

d. Robert lost his cell phone on the BUS this morning.

e. Robert lost his cell phone on the bus THIS MORNING.

Chapter Test 5, Part A

1. For your next vacation, do you plan to travel by plane, by train, or by car?

2. What would you like to drink: water, juice, or soda?

Chapter Test 6, Part A

NOTE TO TEACHER: Make sure to read the boldfaced words with reduced pronunciation, as indicated below.

Cassini-Huygens is the name of a space mission intended to study the planet Saturn. Its spacecraft entered into orbit around Saturn on July 1, 2004, and has been sending back photographs and scientific information since then. One question scientists are investigating is how Saturn got its rings. One theory is that a meteor (1) **might've hit** one of Saturn's moons and shattered it into tiny pieces that began orbiting the planet independently. Scientists never (2) **would've made** this discovery without the use of high-powered telescopes positioned on the spacecraft.

Meanwhile, here on Earth, astronomers are doing research on planets that (3) **could be** habitable. Using computer models, the scientists have calculated the existence of at least 200 planets that (4) **could have** liquid water and an atmosphere—conditions considered necessary for life.

In August of 2006, archaeologists in China discovered dinosaur fossils similar to ones found earlier in North America. The discovery raises the possibility that millions of years ago, Asia and North America (5) **may've been** connected.

Chapter Test 6, Part B

NOTE TO TEACHER: Make sure to read the sentences with reduced pronunciation, as indicated below.

1. My new neighbors are **kinda** strange.

2. My husband's **gra'mother** loves to tell **int'restin'** stories about her family.

3. I'm **gonna** have a piece **a** chocolate.

4. Sorry, I **din'** hear your **firs'** name.

5. I **woulda** come to your party, but I couldn't find a ride.

6. I **don' know** when they **lef'** for the airport.

Chapter Test 7, Part B

NOTE TO TEACHER: Be sure to link sounds where indicated by arcs.

1. Who went‿with you?

2. They‿aren't home.

3. the‿intersection of A and B streets

4. I enjoy‿your singing.

Chapter Test 8, Part A

NOTE TO TEACHER: Be sure to use voiceless pronunciation of "with" for the test.

1. Thursday /θ/

2. rather /ð/

3. there's /ð/

4. with /θ/

5. throat /θ/

CHAPTER 1

A. 10 points (1 point each)

1.	compromise	6.	bizarre
2.	judgmental	7.	euphoric
3.	minimize	8.	debt
4.	adolescence	9.	stages
5.	overreact	10.	stunned

B. 10 points (1 point each)

1. come into contact
2. switch gears
3. gave notice
4. entry level
5. started out
6. get my act together
7. come about, out of the blue
8. support system
9. In retrospect

C. 4 points ($\frac{1}{2}$ point for each boldfaced word)

1. <u>After</u> I **graduate** I'd <u>like</u> to <u>travel</u> in **Africa** for a <u>year</u>.
2. **George** was <u>depressed</u> for <u>months</u> after his **company** <u>transferred</u> him to **Washington**.
3. **That's** the most **amazing** <u>thing</u> I **ever** <u>heard</u>.

D. 5 points (1 point each)

1. still live at
2. when a, becomes an adult

E. 5 points (1 point each)

1. d   2. əd   3. t   4. d   5. d

F. 8 points (2 points for each correct expression)

1. **Man:** Guess what! / Surprise! / I've got good news. / Are you sitting down? / You won't believe this, but . . .

Friend: I'm [thrilled, delighted, happy] for you / Congratulations / That's [great, fantastic / awesome, amazing, wonderful, etc.]

2. **B:** the bad news is / the downside is
   A: I'm sorry to hear that / How awful / What a bummer / That's too bad.

G. 8 points (2 points for each correct use of an expression)

(Paragraphs will vary.) For example:

Last year I graduated from college and needed to find a new place to live. I really wanted to live alone. I <u>started out</u> looking for a one-bedroom apartment, but the prices were very high. I realized I would need to <u>adjust</u> my expectations a bit, so then I looked at a few single apartments. But these were also too expensive. Finally, I <u>changed my mind</u> about living alone and decided to move in with a friend who needed a roommate. <u>In retrospect,</u> this was a smart decision because he introduced me to the woman who is now my fiancée.

CHAPTER 2

A. 15 points (1 point each)

1.	in the habit	9.	brainstorming
2.	have an ear	10.	rehearse
3.	tailored	11.	easier said than done
4.	pet peeves		
5.	session	12.	Smog
6.	accommodate	13.	options
7.	on the fence	14.	fitting in
8.	idiomatic	15.	picked up

B. 4 points (2 points for each correct use of an expression)

(Answers will vary, but should use some of these expressions.)

1. Let me make sure I understand this. / So what you're saying is . . . / You said . . .
2. Did you say / Do you mean / You said

C. 4 points (2 points for each correct use
of an expression)

*(Answers will vary, but should use some of these
expressions.)*

1. My point is / What I'm getting at is / What
   I'm trying to say is / What this means is / In
   other words
2. (Same as number 1.)

D. 5 points (1 point each)

1. falling   4. falling
2. rising   5. rising
3. flat

E. 5 points (1 point each slash)

1. She works in the university library / from 3
   to 6 P.M. / Tuesday to Sunday.
2. I have no idea / where my daughter went / or
   who she's with.
3. The boy's shoes are too small / and his pants
   are too short.

F. 7 points (1 point each)

A: I got a TICKET today.
B: What FOR?
A: I FORGOT to put MONEY in the PARKING
   meter.
B: THAT'S a SHAME.

G. 4 points (1 point each)

1. b   2. d   3. e   4. a

H. 6 points (2 points for each correct
reason or example)

(Answers will vary.) For example:

Formal learner: Attends class, studies grammar
rules, memorizes vocabulary lists, makes flash
cards, learns from a book
Natural learner: Makes friends with native speakers,
listens to songs, watches TV, uses the new language
in everyday life, listens to people and imitates them,
picks up the language by listening, uses the language
in every possible situation

CHAPTER 3

A. 4 points (1 point each)

1. rising   3. rising
2. falling   4. falling

B. 4 points ($\frac{1}{2}$ point each)

1. back, student, loans
2. service, minimum, balance
3. broke, down

C. 10 points (2 points per line)

*(Answers will vary, but should contain this
information)*
Av. Am. = $8,000 in cred. card debt
However, no. is incorrect
In fact: 25% of Am. have no cred. cards
         31% pay off cred. cards each mo.
         56% of Am. have no cred. card debt

D. 4 points (1 point each)

*(Answers will vary, but should use some of these
expressions.)*

1. increased: rose, went up, skyrocketed,
   jumped
   increase: jump, rise
2. decrease by 50 percent: drop by half
3. decreased: plunged, plummeted, dropped,
   crashed, declined, gone down

E. 10 points (1 point each)

1. deadline
2. waived
3. itemize, cut back
4. balance
5. coupons
6. laid off, make ends meet
7. doubled
8. appropriate

F. 10 points (1 point each)

1. grant
2. paid back, kiss off

3. impact
4. live within their means
5. segment
6. pay off
7. gets by
8. come up short
9. garage sale

G. 8 points (2 points for each correct word)

(Answers will vary.) For example:

I would certainly *lend* money to a relative who needed it because I think family members have a responsibility to help one another. If I needed money, I would not be ashamed to *borrow* it from one of my relatives, and I would do my best to *pay back* the money as quickly as possible. In my culture it is very common for people to give *loans* to their relatives.

I think it is a very bad idea to *lend* money to relatives. Many family relationships have been destroyed because one family member *borrowed* money from another and then could not *pay* it *back*. If a relative of mine was in *debt*, I would tell them to cut back on their spending and *do without* luxuries.

CHAPTER 4

A. 5 points (1 point each)

1. d   3. a   5. e
2. c   4. b

B. 10 points (2 points for each correct use of an expression)

(Answers will vary, but should include some of these expressions.)

1. apologizing: I apologize / I'm sorry / Please forgive me / I didn't mean to do it / It won't happen again
forgiving: I forgive you / That's OK / That's all right / Don't worry about it / Forget about it

reconciling: Let me make it up to you / I feel really bad about this
2. apologizing: I apologize / I'm sorry / Forgive me
forgiving: I forgive you / That's OK / That's all right / Don't worry about it / Forget about it

C. 4 points (1 point for each correct phrase)

1. (Let's) Suppose / Pretend / Imagine / Say
2. (Same as number 1.)
3. What if . . .
4. (Same as number 1.)

D. 5 points (1 point each)

trigger, bring back
elaborate, extend
stage, phase
modify, transform
visualize, picture

E. 10 points (1 point each)

1. sequence
2. slipped my mind
3. absentmindedness
4. facilitate
5. on your mind
6. mind's eye
7. evocative
8. the end of the world
9. scatterbrain
10. systematic

F. 3 points (1 point each)

a, c, f

G. 4 points

(Answers will vary.) A complete answer will include a metaphor and how this metaphor is similar to the way memory works.
For example:
Memory is like a file cabinet / a computer / a DVD / a bulletin board /a roadmap / a warehouse / a library / a closet / a desk.

H. 3 points

(Answers will vary.) A complete answer will include the memory and what triggers it.

I. 6 points

(Answers will vary.) A complete answer will include the target word, its definition, a keyword, and an image to link the keyword with the meaning of the word.

CHAPTER 5

A. 6 points (1 point each)

1. plane ↑   train ↑   car ↓

2. water ↑   juice ↑   soda ↓

B. 4 points (2 points for each correct use of expression)

The following expressions fit both items:
I understand how you feel / I know what you mean / I hear what you're saying / I hear you / I'm with you

C. 6 points (2 points each)

The following expressions fit all items:
all in all, on the whole, generally, in general, for the most part

D. 5 points (1 point each)

1. definitely / absolutely / certainly / no question about it / there is no doubt in my mind
2. I guess / I suppose / I think so / possibly / maybe / perhaps
3. (Same as number 1.)
4. Yes / Yeah / Uh-huh
5. (Same as number 2.)

E. 5 points (1 point each)

1. R   3. I   5. I
2. D   4. M

F. 4 points (1 point each)

1. but / whereas
2. contrasts with
3. In contrast / However / On the other hand / Conversely
4. in contrast / however / on the other hand / conversely

G. 10 points (1 point each)

1. self-esteem
2. accounts
3. washed out
4. distorted
5. fired up
6. thought . . . through
7. in great shape
8. fit in
9. boost
10. a hard time

H. 10 points (1 point each)

1. conducting
2. get ahead
3. run . . . by
4. bulked up
5. on their own
6. disorder
7. analyze
8. bump
9. handwriting is on the wall
10. for a change

CHAPTER 6

A. 10 points (2 points each)

1. might have hit
2. would have made
3. could be
4. could have
5. may have been

B. 10 points (1 point each)

1. My new neighbors are <u>kind of</u> strange.
2. My husband's <u>grandmother</u> loves to tell <u>interesting</u> stories about her family.
3. I'm <u>going</u> to have a piece <u>of</u> chocolate.
4. Sorry, I <u>didn't</u> hear your <u>first name</u>.
5. I <u>would have</u> come to your party, but I couldn't find a ride.
6. I <u>don't know</u> when they <u>left</u> for the airport.

C. 6 points (2 points each)

(Answers will vary.) For example:

1. (False) You can't be serious.
2. (True) You don't honestly believe that, do you?
3. (False) That's ridiculous.

D. 3 points (1 point each)

(Answers will vary.) For example:

1. Anyway
2. at any rate
3. in any case

E. 9 points (3 points for each correct use of an expression)

(Answers will vary.) For example:

1. **We know this because** sea temperatures have risen 0.5°C over the past forty years.
2. **According to** a team led by Ruth Curry of the Woods Hole Oceanographic Institution in Massachusetts, 20,000 square kilometers of freshwater ice melted in the Arctic between 1965 and 1995.
3. **The evidence is clear that** a vast frozen area in Western Siberia is undergoing its first thaw since the end of the Ice Age, 11,000 years ago.

F. 12 points (1 point each)

1. drop in the bucket
2. gut feeling
3. distinctive
4. appraised
5. commodities
6. obsession
7. site
8. fake
9. sharp as a tack
10. funding
11. run of the mill
12. initiated

CHAPTER 7

A. 6 points (2 points each)

(Answers will vary.) For example:

1. My heart goes out to her. / Poor woman. / I feel really bad for her.
2. Yes, bless his heart. / Poor man.
3. I feel sorry for them. / I feel really bad for you.

B. 5 points (1 point each)

1. Who went with you?
2. They aren't home.
3. the intersection of A and B streets
4. I enjoy your singing.

C. 5 points (1 point each)

1. c   3. a   5. b
2. a   4. b

D. 6 points (3 points for each correct sentence)

(Answers will vary.) For example:

1. Initially, I thought the history professor was really strict and demanding. I didn't like his class. But after going over it in my mind, I realized he was just trying to treat us like adults. Now, I think he's an excellent teacher.
2. Originally, I was going to buy a car because it's convenient to have one. But after going over it in my mind, I decided not to do it because it's really hard to find parking around here, and gas is expensive.

E. 8 points (2 points each)

(Answers will vary.) For example:

1. Requiring gun owners to take a gun-safety course resulted in a reduction in the number of gun-related accidents.
2. A reduction in the number of gun-related accidents was the result of requiring gun owners to take a gun-safety course.
3. Requiring gun owners to take a gun-safety course led to a reduction in the number of gun-related accidents.
4. A reduction in the number of gun-related accidents was caused by requiring gun owners to take a gun-safety course.

F. 5 points (1 point each)

1. b   3. h   5. f
2. c   4. a

G. 10 points (1 point each)

1. deliberated
2. erode
3. evidence
4. ended up
5. infuriated
6. violation
7. make
8. testified
9. empowered
10. generate

H. 6 points (2 points for each correct word. You may choose to give students extra credit if they use more than three of the words in the list.)

(Paragraphs will vary.) For example:

I work downtown, but I have never seen panhandlers <u>threaten</u> anybody. Still, I know that some people find them <u>menacing</u>. I don't believe panhandlers should be <u>arrested</u>, but I think it is fair to pass an <u>ordinance</u> that <u>keeps them away from</u> business and tourist areas. Panhandlers are human beings and it is unfortunate that they have to beg in order to survive, but their needs should be balanced against the right of downtown visitors to feel safe and comfortable.

CHAPTER 8

A. 5 points (1 point each)

	Voiceless /θ/	Voiced /ð/
1.	Thursday	
2.		rather
3.		there's
4.	with	
5.	throat	

B. 5 points (1 point each)

1. flop
2. unbearably
3. grating
4. inconsistent
5. mishandled

C. 8 points (2 points each)

(Answers will vary.) For example:

1. A feature film is a full-length movie, usually about 90 to 120 minutes in length.
2. The music for a movie or television show is called the film score.
3. A gaffer is what we call the chief electrician, who is the person responsible for the lighting on a movie set.
4. An animated film that is not of feature length is known as a cartoon.

D. 12 points (3 points for each correct use of an idiom)

(Answers will vary.) For example:

1. Several years ago, I missed out on a really great job opportunity. It was in New York, and I turned it down because I didn't want to leave my boyfriend in Texas. Well, my boyfriend and I broke up, and I'm stuck in a really boring job.
2. I met my wife because I was in the right place at the right time. My friend invited me to a baseball game, and I almost didn't go because I don't like baseball much. At the last minute I agreed to go, and I met my wife because she was sitting next to me at the game.
3. Normally I don't like eating fish, but last week I went to a restaurant with some friends, and they persuaded me to take a chance on ordering the sea bass. And it was delicious!
4. I had the time of my life the last time I went skiing. I went to Mammoth Mountain in California, and everything was perfect.

E. 10 points (1 point each)

1. h
2. g
3. j
4. c
5. f
6. d
7. i
8. a
9. b
10. e

F. 10 points (1 point each)

1. eccentric
2. in sync
3. multitasking
4. Q and A
5. swear word
6. falls apart
7. components
8. iffy
9. ambient
10. take a shot